I've been a pastor for almost four decades and [...]
tion the best Bible reading plan I've run acros[...]
　　　—Mark Atteberry, pastor and aw[...]
　　　　　　　　　　　Dream and *So [...]*

Diane Stortz has taken the concept of reading the [...]
whole new level. She's created a wonderful companion to help women
explore the Bible in a small-group setting that inspires and delights. I
love how she's organized the reading assignments, the weekly sections,
and checkpoints that make the journey through God's Word rich and
alive! I'm looking forward to using this wonderful guide to enrich my
daily time seeking God's heart.

　　　　　　　　　—Dineen Miller, author of *Winning Him*
　　　　　　　　　　　Without Words and *The Soul Saver*

I am impressed with *A Woman's Guide to Reading the Bible in a
Year*. The thoroughness and grace throughout is stunning! Diane has
researched and compiled a resource that provides clear direction for
soaking in God's transforming Word. I can't wait to put this to use
personally and in ministry.

　　　　　　　　—Donna Pyle, founder of Artesian Ministries
　　　　　　　　　　and author of *The God of All Comfort*

Diane Stortz has provided a delightfully engaging and very helpful
guide. I know many women who have been longing for a book just
like this!

　　　　　　—Laurie Aker, author, speaker, Bible teacher, and founder
　　　　　　　　of Thistlebend Ministries, Louisville, Kentucky

This book masterfully connects history and prophecy of the Old Testament with the fulfillment of victory in the New Testament. The
format is simple for individuals and motivating for group studies. It is
powerful to see how God has moved in the circumstances of Diane's life
to lead her and others to a profound understanding of the Scriptures.

　　　　　—Dee Ann Turner, vice president, corporate talent, Chick-fil-A

With a unique gift of insight, Diane Stortz makes reading through the
Bible manageable and exciting. This book will have a powerful impact
in your life if you accept her invitation to journey through the Word.

　　　　　　—Linda Mirante, director of women's ministries and adult
　　　　education, Bachelor Creek Church of Christ, Wabash, Indiana;
　　　trustee, Cincinnati Christian University; and inspirational speaker.

A Woman's Guide to Reading the Bible in a Year is a wonderful tool for women wanting to read and understand the Bible. The personal testimony is so relevant for today's busy women. An excellent small-group study guide with biblical history and factual information to enhance the reading plan.

—Patricia Rohach, director of women's ministry,
NorthEast Christian Church, Lexington, Kentucky;
founder and director, Women In Service for Christ

As a Bible study teacher and lecturer for over thirty years, I can attest to the fact that reading the Word of God with a systematic plan helps you to know not only your Bible and God's plan for his creation, but also to know your God in a personal way. Diane Stortz has presented a plan that is easy to follow and yields great rewards as you are guided to think about and meditate on what you read each week.

—Carol Martin, coordinator, People of the Word Bible
Study, Eastside Christian Church, Fullerton, California

Diane's passion for the Word is eclipsed only by her passion for the One who breathed it. The simplicity and warmth of her style makes the daily readings personal. Is there anything more powerful than a friend who's "with you"? I'm honored to call Diane a colleague, a mentor, my lifetime friend.

—Robin M. Stanley, speaker, writer,
life coach, and publishing consultant

Reading the whole of Scripture in the way laid out in this book lays a foundation . . . to be strengthened, expanded, and built upon throughout life. Diane gently takes her readers' hands . . . and . . . gives those hands to our God, who will write on their hearts. Her chapter notes and checkpoints give tools to dig into the Scripture while not overwhelming the reader. . . . If you are going to endeavor to read the whole of Scripture in a year, then let Diane's book be your first of many.

—Michael Dean, involvement minister,
First Christian Church, Albuquerque, New Mexico

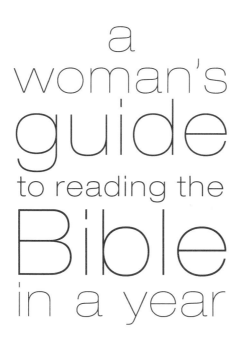

a woman's guide to reading the Bible in a year

a life-changing journey into the heart of God

Diane Stortz

BETHANYHOUSE

a division of Baker Publishing Group
Minneapolis, Minnesota

© 2013 by Diane Stortz

Published by Bethany House Publishers
11400 Hampshire Avenue South
Bloomington, Minnesota 55438
www.bethanyhouse.com

Bethany House Publishers is a division of
Baker Publishing Group, Grand Rapids, Michigan

Printed in the United States of America

Library of Congress Cataloging-in-Publication Data
Stortz, Diane M.
    A woman's guide to reading the Bible in a year : a life-changing journey into the heart of God / Diane Stortz.
        p.   cm.
    Includes bibliographical references.
    ISBN 978-0-7642-1073-0 (pbk. : alk. paper)
    1. Bible—Introductions. 2. Bible—Reading. I. Title.
BS475.3.S75 2013
220.6′1—dc23   2012034672

Cover design by Brand Navigation

Author is represented by Books & Such Literary Agency

20   21   22   23   24   25   14   13   12   11   10   9

For Beth Hawkins Neuenschwander
and all the Monday night Bible study ladies

contents

stories of the journey

You want to read the Bible, but you're afraid you won't understand it.

You've tried to read through the Bible before, but you gave up in the middle of Leviticus.

You're not sure about the Christian faith, but you're looking for answers.

You've been a Christian for many years, but you've never read some parts of the Bible.

You want to know what God says in the Bible, but you don't have a lot of time.

You want to improve your life, but you're not sure God can do anything to help.

Do any of these descriptions apply to you? Then join with other women in situations just like yours who've made an amazing discovery: Reading through the Bible in a year and meeting with others to talk over what you've read can be a life-changing journey, straight into the heart of God!

On the first Monday night of a new year more than a decade ago, I sat with sixteen other women in the cheerful living room of an acquaintance from my church who was starting a new women's group.

"We're here to get to know God by reading through the Bible in a year," Beth said. "We'll read about three chapters a day and meet each week to discuss what we've read." I took a deep breath and silently thanked God for getting me to Beth's house safely, despite a raging thunderstorm that almost kept me home. I knew I was supposed to be right where I was.

Over the next ten years, the group that formed that night met continuously. It spun off two ongoing women's groups and inspired a lively men's breakfast group as well. More than one hundred women have participated, most for multiple years. Along with me, they gladly testify to the benefits and life-changing power of getting to know God through reading and discussing his Word—*all* of his Word—together.

Women like Marlene, a single mom of three on a search for truth.

Women like Liz, a young wife and mom who wanted a happier marriage.

Women like Lynn, a former missionary faced with serious life setbacks.

Women like me, struggling to succeed at life under the heavy weight of feeling inadequate and alone.

And many more. Together we've learned that reading the Bible to get to know God leads to life changes with significant impact.

The Bible reveals God to us. Tullian Tchividjian writes, "The Bible tells one story and points to one figure: It tells the story of how God rescues a broken world and points to Christ who accomplishes this."[1]

God can and does speak to us sometimes in other ways, but in the Bible we can hear God's voice anytime. In the Bible we can see what God does, how he acts. In the Bible we can learn how he has proven that he is loving, faithful, mighty, and true. In the Bible we discover the life-giving power of the living words of God.

1. http://thegospelcoalition.org/blogs/tgc/2009/12/28/what-the-bible-is-not

God put the Bible together for you. He wants you to read it, and you can! A little help to get started and a little encouragement to keep going are all you need. That's what this guidebook and a group of women can provide.

And like me and the other women who've already embarked on this journey, you'll discover the heart of God—and you will never be the same.

You Can Find Truth—and Love

With a Catholic upbringing and years of studying with Jehovah's Witnesses, Marlene joined the Monday night Bible study at Beth's home shortly after her brother died unexpectedly. A single mom of three, Marlene had been searching for something for a long time.

"I grew up knowing the Bible was absolutely the Word of God," she says. "I knew the major Bible stories. I knew Jesus was God's Son. I also knew something was missing." Watching the crowds at Billy Graham crusades on TV underscored this suspicion. "There were always a lot of people crying and raising their hands toward heaven. What was that? I knew it was some kind of love for Jesus that I didn't have."

Jehovah's Witnesses got Marlene reading the Bible. "The Jehovah's Witnesses taught me a lot of things that were different from how I had been raised," she says. "They wanted me to read *their* Bible, but I read the one I had. The problem was, none of it made sense! Now I was confused. Was Jesus God or not? I always thought so. Was the Holy Spirit part of the Trinity or not? I didn't have time to figure all that out. I had three babies and a horrible marriage. I talked to God all the time, and yet he was always somewhere in the background. There was something so empty in my life. Something so wrong. Something was missing!"

When her marriage ended, Marlene says, "the pain was unbearable. No one and nothing was helping. I knew I was in real trouble. At some point it hit me that only God could help. I had asked him for help before, but this was different." Beginning to feel a need to draw closer to God and to know Jesus, Marlene began a search for a church. "God led me to an amazing church. There, I learned what was missing: a relationship. I realized I knew *about* Jesus, but did I know *him*?"

Marlene attended worship every week and began serving with a ministry to homeless people. But she put off joining a small group—until her brother died. "It was devastating," she says. "Something about that opened the void more. I think I wanted answers."

That's when Marlene joined a group of women reading through the Bible in a year. "It has utterly changed my life. There were many different types of women there. Some were new, like me, and others had walked with the Lord a very long time. This was all very much out of my comfort zone, and I felt a little intimidated. There was no need. I soon realized how safe and accepted I was there.

"I started learning things right away. Slowly, the things that confused me about God's Word started making sense. He tells us that sometimes he hides things until we're ready and seeking sincerely.

"This is my tenth year reading through the Bible. It is a commitment; it is a privilege. I tell my children that you become the company you keep. Being in the Word is how we 'hang out' with Jesus. And I hope and pray to become more and more like the women God has put in my life. They are helping to mold me into the woman God wants me to be. They are one of the reasons I know God loves me so much.

"I was lost; through God's Word I have been found. He has set my feet on a solid foundation. Finding Jesus through the Word has brought me to the most fulfilling, loving, intimate, safe relationship I will ever have. I will have it for all eternity. It's the love I've looked for all my life. That void in my heart? It's been filled!"

✎ You Can Find Direction—and Peace

Liz, now a homeschooling mom of six, first realized something wasn't right in her relationship with her husband not long after their first child was born. "We were visiting friends, and I asked Doug to bring me something for the baby. He told me I could get it myself. My friend commented on what a change that was. At one time Doug would have done anything for me."

Looking back, Liz says, "When Doug and I were first married, I was very strong willed and a new Christian. I didn't yet realize all God had in store for me. I was raised in a home where my mom was the head and somewhat cutting to my dad, although she loved him and was a good mom. But that was my model, and Doug was so tenderhearted and kind that it was easy to try to take charge and put him in his place. I didn't know anything different."

After her friend's remark, Liz was more aware of her circumstances. Some time went by, however, before she was enveloped in God's Word and surrounded by women striving to be godly in their marriages. Liz says that when she joined a group of women who were reading through the Bible in a year, she began seeing who God is and what he says in his Word in its entirety. "God started working on my heart," she says. "I started seeing how a woman should treat her husband and her marriage and that I had not been glorifying God or respecting my husband in my actions and words."

Liz began making changes. "I stopped venting to family and friends about the grievances I had toward my husband. Instead I talked to God about them and I also talked to Doug about my feelings. I started viewing my husband and my marriage the way God did—with respect and affection. I also changed how I talked about my husband to *myself*. When he did something I took offense to, I didn't belittle him in my mind—I prayed. I recalled what Scripture had taught me, and I found I wasn't as angry at him or didn't hold on to the hurts as long."

The Bible, Liz says, was pivotal in helping her and her husband "figure out the proper priorities in our marriage and not fall prey to what the world would suggest." Liz also puts her new knowledge toward helping her daughters and other young girls grow into women who know God's Word. Twice a month she hosts and teaches a Girls Gone Wise club in her home. "I have found obeying God to bring great joy and much harmony in my marriage—in my life."

You Can Find Assurance—and Help in Trouble

When Lynn served as a missionary in Japan with her husband thirty years ago, she read through the Bible a couple of times on her own. "I just knew that I wasn't in the Word enough—trying to teach people about the Bible but not reading it enough myself. I'd also been in some discussions and realized I wasn't clear on certain key doctrines and not as familiar with the Scriptures as I should be."

Later Lynn and her family were forced to return to the States under very difficult circumstances. "Although we depended on God to help us get reestablished and settled," Lynn recalls, "I shook constantly, felt ill, cried easily, and couldn't focus. Some days were so bad a little timer was required to pull me through the schedule. Ten minutes cleaning . . . PING. Ten minutes paying the bills . . . PING. Ten minutes crying . . . PING. On many days I sat down with an open Bible—a small, symbolic act of defiance against the enemy. I could only hope that merely holding the Bible for ten minutes would release some sort of magic cure."

And then one day, Lynn turned to Psalm 119. "This long song of praise that God's Word is true cured a deep depression when I couldn't grab on to anything else. It seemed strange to select the longest chapter in the Bible, but God had prescribed the correct medicine. The first 147 verses were rough going. Then, almost imperceptibly, I began to relax. A few rare and precious moments of peace prevailed as I actually zeroed in on the final portion. For the first time in weeks, I felt a little better. And the relief remained for hours."

Lynn read Psalm 119 aloud once each day over the next month. "It was almost as if I were both hearing the Lord's words and repeating them back to him: 'Your Word is true, Your Word is true' . . . 176 times."

A few years later, Lynn's husband died suddenly. "I knew I needed to be in the Word and needed to be around people," she says. Lynn joined the group of women reading through the Bible in a year at Beth's. "One of the best—and most amazing—parts of this experience was watching the Bible speak to women whether they were long-time or first-time readers. How wonderful to hear insights and questions and applications from women at various stages of their walk with the Lord, perspectives I'd never thought of.

"Reading with others is great!" Lynn continues. "You want to make progress every week, and the group means accountability—sort of like Weight Watchers! And as I read through in a given year, Scriptures that relate to the current issues jump out, often as if I'm seeing them for the first time. I'm continually astounded that the Bible has so much to say about any given subject."

Although no longer serving as a missionary on the field, Lynn runs a website dedicated to supporting and encouraging ongoing mission work in Japan. She also writes and teaches to help Christians assess spiritual teaching in light of Scripture. She says that as she reads the Bible now, she can look back on life experiences "as they related to what God promised, how he led, how right he was. That brings such comfort and strength. The more you read, the more you understand the whys and wherefores, and the more you see God's fathomless mercy and love mingled with all that power."

You Can Find Healing—and Release

Remember me at the start of this chapter, sitting in Beth's living room and thanking God for getting me there?

I was born with just one fully formed hip socket instead of two, a condition that went undetected until I began to walk sometime after my first birthday. Then my lopsided gait made clear that something was wrong. (For years now, newborns have been checked routinely for this condition, but this was the early 1950s.) Doctors told my parents about a new treatment at that time: The ball of my thigh bone could be pressed against my stump of a hip socket, and the pressure would stimulate the socket bone to grow. I'd be in full body casts for a year or more to keep the bones in place. First, though, I had to stay in the hospital in traction. I was about fifteen months old, and in those days parents were not allowed to stay with children overnight in the hospital.

I don't have any memories of that hospital time, and I'm ever so thankful the treatment worked and the bone grew. After the casts I wore braces, but eventually I could walk normally. A sense of aloneness seemed to follow me as I grew up, however. I had missed out on several years of developmental play, and I wasn't as strong or well coordinated as other children my age. In elementary school I began to feel different and left out, and sometimes a separation caused an unexplainable deep sadness—even terror. As I grew up, my parents let me try a variety of activities and praised my academic accomplishments, but I never felt adequate compared to my peers. And I never told anyone how I felt.

Despite doing adult things—completing college, moving across the country, finding a job, getting married, having children, and succeeding professionally—I didn't feel like an adult. Connecting deeply with others was hard. People thought I was reserved, private. In reality I was struggling. Much of the time I didn't even know it. Other times I cried out to God to do something. Looking back, I can see that God held me firmly in his hands, and when *I* was finally ready to "do something," he answered my cries for help.

A women's group—Beth's group—was forming to read through the Bible in a year. I thought I would like to do that, and I thought maybe I'd find a friend. I even bravely said I was looking for friends as we introduced ourselves to the rest of the group.

I discovered I loved reading the Bible. I loved how promises of God being for us and with us jumped out. There was a lot I didn't understand that first year, but I felt accepted and safe in this group of women. I discovered I could make friends. But then life got complicated, and I eventually recognized I was depressed. I found and started meeting with a professional Christian counselor, which I don't think I could have done without the filling up and sense of connection that had come from reading through the Bible with my friends.

With my counselor I began to unpack my life, and I discovered that what I needed to have and do to be emotionally healthy is rooted right in the Bible. God models good boundaries and strong connections by how he conducts himself, and his instructions tell us how to make life work. As the Creator of our lives, he knows!

Then, as I continued reading through the Bible with my group, I began to see not only God's guidelines and principles but God himself—his holiness, his power, his faithfulness, his sovereignty, his justice, his love—his heart. Though I occasionally struggle with regret about the years I could have been a different daughter, wife, mother, and friend, I'm focused now on the present and the future. When we change how we think and what we do, we write new endings to our stories! That's what God wants, and he shows us why and how throughout the pages of his story, the Bible.

What Does Your Journey Hold?

Other women who've read through the Bible with a group have shared with me what was important about the experience for them:

I'm able to see how things fall into place. The change in me is trusting God for everything.

—Iona

I keep on because it provides accountability for staying in the Word, because I see growth not only in myself but in the other women I've come to know, and because I love those women and enjoy being with them on a regular basis. If we stay focused and seek God's heart and message to us personally, reading the Word repeatedly never gets old!

—Donna

I wish I'd done this twenty years ago. It has given me a better understanding of myself. And it's been a long time now since I've heard a sermon and not already been familiar with the Scripture being talked about. The answers to everything are right here in the Bible, but you have to read it to get it.

—Jan

Reading through the Bible absolutely changed my life. Reading and discussing it with others made the Word of God *alive*! It brought me into a *relationship* with our Father. It's indescribable!

—MaryJo

I've learned not to be so independent. I've learned the value of sharing my experiences with others, of prayer, of being prayed for, of being part of a group that does not judge.

—Jeanette

Reading through the Bible this year with my group, we came to the Old Testament book of Job. I finally saw that suffering is a part of everyone's earthly life. The suffering I had endured did not necessarily mean that I had been its cause or even that I had deserved it. I don't know why it took me forty-five years to see this truth. All I know is that God used his Word and this women's Bible study to heal my heart completely.

—Jo

I had tried to read the Bible before. Incest, murder, lying, deception! Who *were* these people? Now I see that it's all part of sin. I've read through the Bible five or six times. Without a group, I never would have read the Bible or appreciated it like I do now. Now it makes sense to me.

—Bev

I was invited by a friend. I went because I needed a group to pray with. The whole group experience, as well as being in the Word, has made my faith and prayer life deeper and more a part of every hour of every day.

—Linda

A habit takes a month or so to establish. Making a commitment to read through the Bible in a year with a group established my habit of spending time each day in the Scriptures. After one year I was hungry to do it again and again!

—Rachel

The woman who invited me to her home to join a group and read through the Bible in a year is Beth Hawkins Neuenschwander. In 2010 Beth moved with her husband and family to a different state and a new ministry. Before she left, she sent an e-mail to everyone who had participated in the group she'd hosted for more than ten years. Part of it said, "You have been the strength and encouragement and laughter and tears I have needed, so thank you, thank you, thank you. . . . The challenge to keep the house clean was nothing compared to the joy that came from giving willing hearts the chance to see God through his Word."

Psalm 119 says, "Give me understanding and I will obey your instructions; I will put them into practice with all my heart. . . . Turn my eyes from worthless things, and give me life through your word" (vv. 34, 37). Is that your prayer? God never turns away anyone who wants to know him better. Let him show you who he is. Find the hope and purpose he wants you to have! "Come close to God, and God will come close to you" (James 4:8).

Welcome to the journey! Let's begin. . . .

how to use
this book

Here are some tips to help you use this book to get the most out of your journey.

- *You can begin your year of reading through the Bible at any time.* The weekly pages are numbered but not dated.
- *You can use this guide with any Bible version.* If you already have a version you like, that's fine. If not, or if you're new to the Bible, consider using one of the newer translations intended for modern readers, such as *God's Word Translation, the Holman Christian Standard Bible, Today's English Version,* or the *New Living Translation.* Be sure to choose an actual translation and not a paraphrase, to keep the focus on hearing from God most directly. If you prefer, you can listen to an audio Bible and follow along. Check out what's available from the online sources listed at the back of this book.

   Whatever Bible you choose or how you choose to read it, you'll want to be able to bring it with you to meetings if you're doing this journey with a group.

- *This guide avoids presenting any particular doctrinal views.* Instead it simply presents a plan and a process for reading the Bible so that in your reading God can speak to you firsthand.

- *For each week of the journey, here's what you'll find in this book:* First, a list of that week's readings and some brief, basic background information. The Checkpoints section lists five interesting objects, events, or people to watch for as you read throughout the week. Use the prompts and writing spaces in the Share the Journey section to record your responses to what you read—what stands out, something you've learned about who God is, a passage or verse you'd like to remember, or any questions you'd like to pursue.

- *On most days you'll read three chapters, which might take fifteen or twenty minutes.* The reading plan for your journey alternates Old Testament and New Testament books through most of the year, with the book of Psalms divided into four parts interspersed among the other books. Since most of us are more familiar with the New Testament than the Old Testament, this plan helps provide momentum to keep you reading throughout the year. Also, you just might find yourself making some amazing connections between the Old and New Testaments as you alternate between them.

- *Think of your reading as a conversation with God.* Think, react, and listen for what God wants to show you. If your Bible provides detailed study notes and you want to explore those, do so *after* the chapters for the day. This will give you an opportunity to interact with the text first on your own to make your own discoveries.

- *There's no right or wrong way to take this journey!* Reading every day helps you establish a habit of setting aside time to hear from God every day. But if you find you need to read only two or three times a week, that's fine too.

- *Nearly everyone sometimes falls behind. When that happens, don't give up!* If catching up seems too daunting, simply pick up at the current spot on the schedule and keep reading.

- *Expect to puzzle over some events and customs, but also expect to develop understanding as you continue to read.* God is good, and there's a purpose for everything included in his Word. You'll be amazed at how much more you'll understand if you simply keep reading to get to know God. His Word will accomplish his goals. He is more than able!

- *Be sure to write something in each week's Share the Journey section,* even if you're working through this book on your own. At the end of the year, you'll have a record of your journey, and you'll be able to see how you've grown in your understanding of who God is.

- *If you can, take the journey with a friend or a small group.* Meeting with others every week to talk over what you've read provides great encouragement and accountability to keep reading throughout the year. In addition, you'll benefit when you hear what God is teaching others as the women in your group share their insights and discoveries.

guidelines for groups

If you're starting a group, facilitating a group, or participating in a group, let this advice from women already on the journey guide you.

- *Set your start date several weeks in advance and communicate the goal clearly:* getting to know God by reading the Bible in a year and meeting weekly to discuss what you've read. You might hold an introductory meeting to explain the journey, make copies of this book available, and allow women who are interested to sign up.
- *Plan to meet year-round.* There might be a time or two that the group decides not to meet because of major holidays. But meeting and discussing the readings is too important—and too enjoyable—to skip the summer months, even though not everyone will be able to attend every week because of vacation travels.
- *If you're starting a new group, put out an open invitation* to the women in your church, moms ministry, workplace, or community and trust God to bring the women who should

attend. It might be a group of peers or a group with varied ages and situations. Either configuration can greatly bless the women who participate.

• *Keep your group size conducive to conversation.* Not everyone will speak up every week, and now and then someone will always be content just to listen. But in a group of more than twelve or so, some members stop contributing to the discussions and others tend to dominate. If your group is large, consider occasionally numbering off and breaking into groups of three or four—some women will participate more in this smaller setting. Or divide into two smaller groups.

• *Let participants choose their own Bible versions.* Try to include at least one translation in modern English. (See the list in the How to Use This Book section.) In your discussions, verses will sometimes be read aloud, and hearing a verse in several translations can help with understanding. Try to avoid paraphrases.

• *Choose a comfortable meeting place and schedule.* Whether you meet in a home, a room in your church, or another location, make sure the size of the room will accommodate everyone comfortably. An evening meeting generally will allow the most women to participate unless child care is provided. Plan for ten or fifteen minutes for women to chat and catch up with one another before your discussion begins. Allow at least an hour for discussion and some additional time for prayer.

If possible, and depending on the season, have hot or cold beverages available. If you'd like, provide occasional snacks as well.

• *Open your discussions with the simple question "What stood out for you in this week's reading?"* That is usually all it takes to start a lively conversation as women share special passages, new ideas, and questions, and respond to what others have to say.

- *Develop an atmosphere where all questions are safe and no one has to have all the answers.* Welcome questions and struggles. Learn from one another. Make it always OK to say "What do you think?" or "I don't know." This is especially important if group members come from a variety of backgrounds. Occasionally someone in the group will want to talk about a special concern. Ask, "What does this passage teach us about God's character?" to refocus the group if the discussion seems to be veering too far from the text.

- *Be comfortable with occasional silence.* Ask, "What else stood out for you?" and wait. Almost always, someone will be prompted to share another point or question. In this way, the Holy Spirit guides the group as you interact with each other and the Word.

- *Build community.* Conversation focused on discovering God in his Word naturally builds meaningful, caring connections and overcomes differences in age, race, and marital status. Deepen that sense of community and belonging by praying together at the end of your group time and serving together as a group when opportunities arise.

- *Have fun.* Now and then, consider a break from your group's meeting routine and plan something different. Have a potluck meal before your discussion time (for example, an Anything-but-Turkey buffet at the meeting after Thanksgiving). Find a DVD production of the story of a biblical character (see the list at the back of this book, and also check Christian bookstores and online) and watch it together, comparing the biblical account with the presentation. Invite your minister or a professor from a local Christian college for a question-and-answer session.

25

the Bible
we read today

The Bible says, "All Scripture is God-breathed" (2 Timothy 3:16 NIV). Over more than 1,500 years, through forty different writers, God directed the writing of the sixty-six books that tell his story and reveal his heart. He also directed the coming together of the books that would eventually form the Bible.

The word *canon* refers to the books that became the Bible. In *How We Got Our Bible*, S. Edward Tesh explains:

> Canonization was not a formal process at all, except that men did set forth a list of the books that already had been recognized and accepted as Scripture. . . . What the early church leaders did was to accept the Old Testament Scriptures that Christ and the apostles had recognized, and then to select the apostolic writing and gather them into the New Testament. Always they recognized the authority of the apostles who were to teach "all things" that Christ had commanded. They included in the New Testament only apostolic writings, that is, writings of the apostles and of the apostolic circle. Any books they rejected were rejected because they did not belong to this group.[2]

2. S. Edward Tesh, *How We Got Our Bible* (Cincinnati, OH: Standard Publishing, 1961), 47–48.

None of the original manuscripts of the books of the Bible have ever been found, but exceedingly careful copies have given scholars and translators a wealth of material to work with and to give us, through the years, the Bible we read today.

All of the books of the Old Testament had been completed and compiled by about 500 BC. Most of the Old Testament was written in Hebrew. For a long time, the oldest copies of the Old Testament were those prepared by a group of Jewish scholars and scribes (expert transcribers) known as the Masoretes. They wanted to safeguard and pass on the purity of the texts in an understandable form. Between about AD 500 and 900, they prepared what is known as the Masoretic Text.

The discovery of the Dead Sea Scrolls in a cave near the Dead Sea in 1947 provided much older scrolls and fragments of scrolls—from 150 or 100 BC—containing many Old Testament books.

The first translation of the Old Testament into another language, Greek, was the Septuagint, completed about 150 BC.

The books of the New Testament, written in Greek, all appeared within about seventy years after the resurrection. As churches multiplied, copies of these books and letters circulated widely.

Two complete copies of the Bible date to about AD 350. These are known as the Vatican Manuscript and the Sinaitic Manuscript. A third copy, the Alexandrian Manuscript, missing some books and parts of books, dates to about AD 400. Each of these is written in Greek.

The Latin Vulgate, with both Old and New Testaments translated into Latin, was completed in AD 405.

As the English language developed, English translations slowly appeared. In about 1382, John Wycliffe completed an English translation from the Latin Vulgate. He was greatly opposed by many who fought to keep the Word of God from ordinary people in their language, but his work survived.

More than a hundred years later, in 1526, William Tyndale translated the New Testament into English from a Greek text prepared by the scholar Erasmus. Because of the religious and political era in which he lived, however, many considered him a heretic. Tyndale eventually also translated parts of the Old Testament from the Hebrew, but he was imprisoned in 1535 and died at the stake in 1536. In 1611, however, when the King James Version of the Bible was published, as much as 85 percent was retained from the work of William Tyndale.

Because languages evolve and our understanding of ancient languages expands, English translations of the Bible continue. Some determine to come as close to a word-for-word translation as possible; others strive for an accurate thought-for-thought equivalence or a combination of these two methods. Depending on the purpose of the translation, some are easier to read than others. Bible publishers often create study notes, devotions, and short informative articles to include in Bibles aimed at a particular audience. Take some time to explore the various Bible translations and presentations available today. You are sure to find one that beckons you to dive in and read!

the books of the Bible

The Bible is actually sixty-six different books, put together to tell one big story. It's helpful to picture the arrangement of the books of the Bible as books arranged on a bookshelf. The Old Testament shelves hold books of law, history, poetry, and prophecy. On the New Testament shelves are the Gospels and books of history, letters, and prophecy.

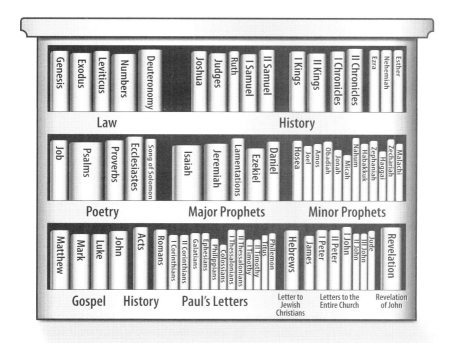

beginnings

The Old Testament (old covenant) of the Bible tells the story of the relationship between God and humanity before the birth of Jesus. Genesis, the first book of the Old Testament, is a book of beginnings: the creation of the world and the first human beings, the development of nations, and the start of the family that would eventually be the Jewish people, chosen by God for a special purpose. Genesis also presents the entrance of sin into the world and its effects on all creation.

God's covenant with Abram (Abraham), beginning in chapter 12, initiates God's plan to bless the world and save humanity through Abraham's family. A covenant was a binding, legal agreement, usually between two people and with promises made by both sides. God's promises to Abraham, however, were unconditional. God would do what he said. Abraham had only to believe and obey.

Genesis is part of the Pentateuch, the first five books of the Bible (also called the books of law), which were written by Moses. The genealogies in Genesis don't necessarily include every generation but show connections and continuity, linking important people or periods.

Read	Checkpoints
☑ Genesis 1–3	• angels and a flaming sword
☑ Genesis 4–6	• a man who didn't die
☑ Genesis 7–9	
☑ Genesis 10–12	• the first rainbow
☑ Genesis 13–15	• heavenly visitors
☑ Genesis 16–18	• a pillar of salt
☑ Genesis 19–21	

Your decision to open the Bible every day to look into the mirror and see truth from God makes you a light in a world filled with much darkness.

—*Catherine Martin*

Share the Journey

How did you experience God's heart in this week's reading?

Something you learned or an insight you gained

Portions of Genesis seem repulsive.
God is truly patient.

A verse or passage you'd like to remember

I'll always love,
"yes; you did laugh."

Questions

Why do some folks seem to encounter harsher punishment/ consequences than others?

31

faithfulness
and deceit

God tested Abraham's faith with the shocking command to sacrifice Isaac, the child of the promise. Though the request made no sense to him, Abraham committed himself to obey, believing that even if his son did die, God would restore Isaac's life (Hebrews 11:17–19). Isaac's submission and God's provision of a ram for the burnt offering foreshadowed the future sacrifice of Jesus on the cross.

Isaac and Rebekah's twin sons (Esau and Jacob) and the sons and daughter Jacob had with Leah and Rachel, Bilhah and Zilpah—the next generations of Abraham's descendants—experienced intrigue, broken relationships, and deceit. Yet God appeared to both Isaac and Jacob and affirmed his covenant promises to Abraham with them. After years in Haran with Rebekah's relatives, Jacob returned home to Canaan a wealthy man and reconciled with his brother. Along the way, God changed Jacob's name to Israel.

Esau's descendants became the nation of Edom, inhabiting the southeastern portion of Canaan. From Jacob's twelve sons, the nation of Israel would grow. And the twelve sons of Ishmael, Abraham's son with Sarah's maid, Hagar, began the people group known today as Arabs.

Read	Checkpoints
☑ Genesis 22–24	• the only land Abraham owned
☑ Genesis 25–27	• birthrights and blessings
☑ Genesis 28–30	• a ladder to heaven
☑ Genesis 31–33	• a special tenth
☑ Genesis 34–36	• dizzying dreams
☑ Genesis 37–39	
☑ Genesis 40–42	

The Spirit breathes upon the Word, and brings the truth to sight.

—William Cowper

Share the Journey

How did you experience God's heart in this week's reading?

Something you learned or an insight you gained

A verse or passage you'd like to remember

Questions

news of a new kingdom

The story of Joseph that began in Genesis 37 concludes in the remaining chapters of that book. Jacob moved to Egypt with his sons and their families and settled in the land of Goshen. When Jacob died, Joseph buried him in Canaan. When Joseph died, his body was entombed in Egypt.

The book of Matthew is the first of four New Testament (new covenant) books known as the Gospels. They record the life of Jesus—his birth, his miracles and teaching, and his death, burial, and resurrection.

Each gospel author communicates the Good News of Jesus with a unique focus. Matthew, Jesus' disciple also known as Levi, wrote to spotlight Jesus as the kingly Messiah (Anointed One, Christ) predicted in the Jewish Scriptures, the Old Testament. Matthew quotes the Old Testament extensively to show how Jesus fulfilled those prophecies.

The genealogy in Matthew provides Jesus' legal lineage through Abraham and David. Mentioning women in a Jewish genealogy was unusual. Even more striking are the stories of the women besides Mary included in the genealogy in chapter 1: Tamar, Rahab, and Bathsheba all sinned sexually (Genesis 38; Joshua 2; 2 Samuel 11–12), and Ruth was a foreigner (Ruth 1:4).

Read	Checkpoints
☑ Genesis 43–45	• a forgiving ruler
☑ Genesis 46–50	• Jesus in Judah's blessing
☑ Matthew 1–3	
☑ Matthew 4–6	• a royal family tree
☑ Matthew 7–9	• a narrow gate
☑ Matthew 10–12	• miracles on land and sea
☑ Matthew 13–15	

The Bible is the cradle wherein Christ is laid.

—Martin Luther

Share the Journey

How did you experience God's heart in this week's reading?

Something you learned or an insight you gained

A verse or passage you'd like to remember

Questions

I AM

As the time for the crucifixion came closer, Jesus began to prepare his disciples. He also acted to solidify their understanding of his identity. He praised Peter for making what we sometimes call the good confession—"You are the Son of God." He took Peter, James, and John up a mountain to see him in heavenly glory with Moses and Elijah (called the transfiguration). Chapter 21 starts Matthew's account of Jesus' last week on earth. By riding into Jerusalem on a donkey, Jesus presented himself publicly as Israel's long-awaited king and Messiah. He continued confronting the Jewish religious leaders and taught with short stories called parables. Matthew's gospel ends with Jesus' last words to his disciples before he returned to heaven.

Jacob's descendants, well settled in Egypt at the end of Genesis, prospered and grew. Egypt's new ruler feared the number of Israelites so much that he made them slaves. From a burning bush in the desert of Midian, God called Moses to lead his people out of Egypt and revealed his name to Moses: I AM, or *Yahweh*. English translations often use the word LORD, with large and small capital letters, to represent God's name.

Read	Checkpoints
☑ Matthew 16–18	• a coin in a fish
☑ Matthew 19–21	• two great commandments
☑ Matthew 22–25	• an alabaster jar
☑ Matthew 26–28	• a ruler's unbelieving heart
☑ Exodus 1–3	• seven plagues
☑ Exodus 4–6	
☑ Exodus 7–9	

When Scripture comes alive in our hearts, it doesn't inform us as much as transform us.

—*Margaret Feinberg*

Share the Journey

How did you experience God's heart in this week's reading?

Something you learned or an insight you gained

A verse or passage you'd like to remember

Questions

a holy nation

The blood of a sacrificial lamb on the doorposts of their homes protected the Israelites from the final plague God brought against Egypt. Then, more than two million strong, with their flocks and herds and with valuable gifts from their Egyptian neighbors, the Israelites hurried out of Egypt.

But even after their release from slavery and their dramatic rescue through the Red Sea, the Israelites had trouble trusting God's care and provision. God continued to show his faithfulness, however. He made a covenant with the entire nation to make them his special people, with a special purpose. He gave the Ten Commandments and the laws found in Exodus 20–23 to describe how his people should live because of their relationship with him.

On the mountain with God, Moses received instructions for the tabernacle, where God would dwell among his people. Everything about the tabernacle's design, furnishings, and care signified God's absolute perfection and holiness. God also described for Moses the special clothing and duties of the priests, who would offer sacrifices for the sins of the people.

Read	Checkpoints
☑ Exodus 10–12	• the Passover lamb
☑ Exodus 13–15	• water from the rock
☑ Exodus 16–18	• a father-in-law's wise advice
☑ Exodus 19–21	• eagles' wings
☑ Exodus 22–24	• a meal on a mountain
☑ Exodus 25–27	
☑ Exodus 28–30	

If I were to go through the Word of God studying only one word, love, I would never get to the end of the wonders.

—Catherine Mackenzie

Share the Journey

How did you experience God's heart in this week's reading?

Something you learned or an insight you gained

A verse or passage you'd like to remember

Questions

no other gods

While Moses was away on the mountain with God, the Israelites demanded other gods to follow. Moses' brother, Aaron, melted down gold jewelry and fashioned an idol from it; he also built an altar. For disobeying the command to worship no one but God, the Israelites experienced consequences, including God's decision that he would not go with his people as they traveled toward the Promised Land. God responded to Moses' pleas for mercy, however, and renewed his covenant with the Israelites. After the tabernacle was set up within the camp, they could always see the cloud of God's presence there—even at night, illuminated by fire.

The gospel of Mark's likely author, mentioned in other New Testament books by the name John Mark, assisted two of the apostles, Peter and Paul, during the early years of the church. A fast-moving book that tracks Jesus' movement from place to place, Mark's gospel focuses on Jesus as teacher, healer, miracle worker, and Savior King. Writing like a reporter for his Gentile (non-Jewish) audience, Mark includes explanations of Jewish customs as well as interesting details of events.

Read	Checkpoints
☑ Exodus 31–33	• twelve precious stones
☑ Exodus 34–36	• a hole in the roof
☐ Exodus 37–40	• a herd of pigs
☑ Mark 1–3	• the eye of a needle
☑ Mark 4–6	• a withered fig tree
☑ Mark 7–9	
☐ Mark 10–12	

The Bible is the only book whose Author is always present when one reads it.

—Anonymous

 **Share the Journey**

How did you experience God's heart in this week's reading?

Something you learned or an insight you gained

A verse or passage you'd like to remember

Questions

41

prophecy and purity

Near the end of Mark's gospel, we read what Jesus told his disciples about the fall of Jerusalem and his second coming. Then, as they celebrated Passover together, Jesus focused on nearer events—his betrayal by one of the Twelve and Peter's three-time denial.

The book of Leviticus takes its name from the tribe of Levi, which provided the priests for the nation of Israel. Leviticus recounts what God told his people to do to maintain the special position he had given them—a holy (set apart) relationship with him. The practices God required can sound odd or even harsh to us, but they illustrated to the Israelites—and show us also—the necessity of holy living and the cost of atonement (reconciliation) and forgiveness. After Aaron and his sons began their work of making sacrifices and presenting the people's offerings, God once again made known his presence among his people.

Distinguishing between clean and unclean and following the other regulations for holy living also set the Israelites apart from other people groups and promoted their health and welfare. As God blessed their holy way of life, other nations would see an example of his power and care.

Read	Checkpoints
☑ Mark 13–16	• an upper room
☑ Leviticus 1–3	• blood and fat
☑ Leviticus 4–6	• a special turban
☑ Leviticus 7–9	• cedar and hyssop
☑ Leviticus 10–12	• the scapegoat
☑ Leviticus 13–15	
☑ Leviticus 16–18	

There's no better book with which to defend the Bible than the Bible itself.

—Dwight L. Moody

Share the Journey

How did you experience God's heart in this week's reading?

Something you learned or an insight you gained

A verse or passage you'd like to remember

Questions

43

reasons for rejoicing

What would life look like as the Israelites lived out their set-apart relationship with God? Leviticus turns its focus to holiness in personal conduct, first for individuals and then for Israel's priests. At specified feasts (festivals) throughout the year, individuals came together to celebrate their relationship with God and thank him for his gifts. Fellow Israelites who sold themselves as slaves were to be treated as hired workers and set free after six years of service (Deuteronomy 15:12) or during the Year of Jubilee, which occurred every fifty years.

The gospel of Luke includes details about Jesus' birth and early years from his mother's perspective, including the encounter at the temple with Simeon and Anna, aged and godly, who recognized baby Jesus as the Savior and rejoiced.

Luke, a Gentile physician, never met Jesus but compiled his account of Jesus' life through careful investigation and interviews (very likely including talks with Mary, Jesus' mother). In a red-letter Bible, much of Luke appears in red type because much of the book directly quotes Jesus' teaching, including many of his parables. Luke also records many of the miracles that supported Jesus' claims of authority.

Read	Checkpoints
☑ Leviticus 19–21	• lamps that never go out
☑ Leviticus 22–24	• time to rest
☑ Leviticus 25–27	
☐ Luke 1–3	• an angel by an altar
☐ Luke 4–6	• nets full of fish
☐ Luke 7–9	• a legion of demons
☐ Luke 10–12	

Knowing the Word of God is your best weapon against the lies that the enemy will tell you.

—*Christy Miller*

Share the Journey

How did you experience God's heart in this week's reading?

Something you learned or an insight you gained

A verse or passage you'd like to remember

Questions

45

ready and waiting

In the second half of his gospel, Luke continues to emphasize that the gospel (the Good News) of the kingdom of God is for the whole world—not just for the Jews. Luke spotlights Jesus' conflict with the Jewish leaders over thinking they could get into the kingdom on their own merits.

Chapter 19 records Jesus entering Jerusalem at the beginning of the week in which he would be crucified. After his death and resurrection, as he was getting ready to return to heaven, Jesus told the disciples to wait in Jerusalem for the coming of the Holy Spirit.

The book of Numbers records important events during the nearly forty years the Israelites traveled and camped around the wilderness of Sinai before the second generation finally entered Canaan, the Promised Land. The first nine chapters describe a census God commanded as well as the orderly organization of the Israelite camp. The detailed lists and numbers in these chapters can sound tedious. But to Israelites living in the ancient world, this record would have had the sound of a glorious celebration of all God had accomplished.

Read	Checkpoints
☑ Luke 13–15	• a great dividing space
☑ Luke 16–18	• a persistent woman
☑ Luke 19–21	
☑ Luke 22–24	• two tiny coins
☐ Numbers 1–3	• an orderly camp
☑ Numbers 4–6	• a priestly blessing
☐ Numbers 7–9	

The Bible is . . . as necessary to spiritual life as breath is to natural life. There is nothing more essential to our lives than the Word of God.

—*Jack Hayford*

Share the Journey

How did you experience God's heart in this week's reading?

Something you learned or an insight you gained

A verse or passage you'd like to remember

Questions

wilderness travails

When their camp was fully organized, God sent the Israelites out to the wilderness of Sinai. They traveled and camped from place to place until God told Moses to send twelve men into the land of Canaan, the Promised Land, to explore it.

After forty days the men returned, carrying samples of amazing produce but dismayed by the size and strength of the people they had seen. Ten of the twelve reported that the Israelites could never take the land. Only Caleb and Joshua disagreed. Fearfully siding with the ten, the Israelites rebelled against God. Their ultimate consequence was nearly forty years of desert wandering. Except for Caleb and Joshua, no one twenty years old or older would ever enter Canaan.

A Levite named Korah and two others gathered 250 followers and incited a rebellion against Moses, but with disastrous results for themselves. With leadership from God through Moses and Aaron restored, the Israelites' journeying continued, and surrounding nations began to consider them a threat. At the same time, although they had been warned against it, the Israelites began to be influenced by the worship of those nations' gods.

Read	Checkpoints
☑ Numbers 10–12	• giants and grasshoppers
☑ Numbers 13–15	• almond buds and blossoms
☑ Numbers 16–18	
☑ Numbers 19–21	• a talking donkey
☑ Numbers 22–24	• a star from Jacob's tribe
☑ Numbers 25–27	• female heirs
☑ Numbers 28–30	

The Bible was written in tears, and to tears it yields its best treasures.

—*A. W. Tozer*

Share the Journey

How did you experience God's heart in this week's reading?

Something you learned or an insight you gained

A verse or passage you'd like to remember

Questions

the way, the truth, and the life

As the Israelites' time of desert wandering concluded, God gave Moses his final tasks. Moses issued to the people God's command to destroy the Midianites, and he negotiated with the tribes of Reuben and Gad about their request to settle on the eastern side of the Jordan River. Moses also conveyed God's instructions for Israel's national boundaries and how tribal boundaries were to be established. Chapter 33 recounts all the places the Israelites camped during their wilderness years.

John's gospel, possibly written around AD 90, differs from the other three gospels in significant ways. It is not chronological, it includes long teaching discourses or sermons by Jesus, and it focuses primarily on Jesus' claim to be God and the evidence that his claim is true. From John's opening remarks to Jesus' seven "I am" statements about himself, from Jesus' miracles (called signs in John) to the testimony of others such as John the Baptist and Martha, this gospel urges readers to believe that Jesus was indeed fully God and fully man, the Son of God, the Jewish Messiah, the Savior of the world.

Read	Checkpoints
☑ Numbers 31–33	• a conversation by a well
☑ Numbers 34–36	• slaves and sons
☑ John 1–3	• the light of the world
☑ John 4–6	• a king on a colt
☑ John 7–9	• a servant's example
☑ John 10–12	
☑ John 13–15	

The Bible is primarily an account of what's wrong with us, of what God planned to do about it, and about what he has done about it in history through the life, death, and resurrection of Jesus Christ.

—*Tim Keller*

Share the Journey

How did you experience God's heart in this week's reading?

Something you learned or an insight you gained

A verse or passage you'd like to remember

Questions

a special treasure

The final chapters of John's gospel include Jesus' prayer for all his followers and then a concise yet detailed account of his arrest, trial, crucifixion, resurrection, and appearances to his disciples. John emphasizes Old Testament prophecies fulfilled and, at the end of chapter 20, summarizes his purpose for writing his book. The final chapter acts as an epilogue; on the shore of the Sea of Galilee—where Jesus had first called Peter to follow him—Peter received Jesus' forgiveness for denying him on the night Jesus was arrested.

Deuteronomy is the last of the five books written by Moses. The title means "second law," but the book is a second telling of God's law given to Moses, not a new or different law. The book records Moses' words to the Israelites while they camped on the east side of the Jordan River, ready to enter the Promised Land. There Moses recounted the Israelites' history with God—from the early covenants through deliverance from slavery in Egypt and the wilderness years—and encouraged the people to be faithful to God and to love and obey him always.

Read	Checkpoints
☑ John 16–18	• lights in a dark olive grove
☑ John 19–21	• a doubting disciple
☑ Deuteronomy 1–3	
☑ Deuteronomy 4–6	• a long iron bed
☐ Deuteronomy 7–9	• doorposts and gates
☑ Deuteronomy 10–12	• a blessing and a curse
☐ Deuteronomy 13–15	

Only one thing validates a message or a messenger: the whole counsel of the Word of God.

—*Kay Arthur*

Share the Journey

How did you experience God's heart in this week's reading?

Something you learned or an insight you gained

A verse or passage you'd like to remember

Questions

choose life!

After Moses reminded the Israelites of their history, he continued to prepare them to enter the Promised Land. In Deuteronomy we read Moses' retelling of much of the law God had given earlier, the terms of his covenant with his people. Then Moses explained how the covenant would be renewed when the people entered the Promised Land. He emphasized God's promises of blessings for obedience but trouble and disaster for disobedience. He prophesied the Israelites' future exile and their return to their land because of God's mercy.

Before his death, Moses wrote down all of God's instructions and gave the book to the priests for safekeeping. He also commanded that all of Deuteronomy be read aloud to the people every seven years. Soon God told Moses to climb Mount Nebo. From there God showed him the entire land of Canaan before he died, and God himself buried Moses. The leadership of God's people then belonged to Joshua.

The book of Psalms contains poetic songs and prayers, written and compiled from the time of Moses to the time of Ezra the scribe, about one thousand years later.

Read	Checkpoints
☐ Deuteronomy 16–18	• a king's handwritten scroll
☐ Deuteronomy 19–21	• sandals that didn't wear out
☐ Deuteronomy 22–24	• choosing life or death
☐ Deuteronomy 25–27	• the view from a mountain
☐ Deuteronomy 28–30	• an unknown burial place
☐ Deuteronomy 31–34	
☐ Psalms 1–5	

It is such a relief to trust God and his Word.
—*Michelle Renihan*

Share the Journey

How did you experience God's heart in this week's reading?

Something you learned or an insight you gained

A verse or passage you'd like to remember

Questions

hear me when I call, O God

The psalms, sung by the Israelites as part of worship at the temple in Jerusalem, express praise to God, pleas for deliverance, and deep emotions of both joy and sorrow. The book of Psalms has five parts, or books, and each one likely was compiled and added at a different time.

The psalms express their authors' responses to the experiences of life. Some of the psalms provide notes about the tune or the instruments to be used with that particular song. These notes often name the author of the psalm and occasionally the event that inspired it. Israel's King David wrote many but not all of the psalms.

Some themes repeat throughout the entire book and provide one way to categorize the psalms. This week's reading contains many examples of psalms of lament or penitence, telling of sorrow for sin and pleading for forgiveness and reconciliation. Wisdom psalms contrast the righteous and the wicked and call on God's people to remember his mighty acts. Royal psalms focus on the coming Messiah. Psalms of praise is a fourth category.

Read	Checkpoints
☑ Psalms 6–10	• talking skies
☑ Psalms 11–15	• hidden and deliberate sins
☑ Psalms 16–20	• an invitation to prayer
☑ Psalms 21–25	• a confident shepherd
☐ Psalms 26–30	• a hiding place and victory songs
☑ Psalms 31–34	
☐ Psalms 35–37	

Psalm 23 has about half as many words as you will find on the back of an aspirin bottle, but it has relieved far more headaches.

—*Dan Schantz*

Share the Journey

How did you experience God's heart in this week's reading?

Something you learned or an insight you gained

A verse or passage you'd like to remember

Questions

power from on high

Four psalms written by King David end the first division of the book of Psalms. They speak of suffering and trial as well as perseverance and praise, with prayers for wisdom. The Hebrew word *selah* comes from the word meaning "to lift up" and is probably a musical notation.

The book of Acts is the history book of the New Testament, recording the beginning and early years of the church and the rapid spread of the Good News. Written by Luke the physician (who also wrote one of the Gospels), Acts begins with Jesus' return to heaven and the coming of the promised Holy Spirit.

The Holy Spirit fills the book of Acts. Much of the first half of the book focuses on Peter, a once-cocky fisherman transformed into a bold and effective leader by the Holy Spirit's power. Then the focus turns to Paul, first known as Saul. A Roman citizen and a Jewish scholar, Saul zealously persecuted Jewish Christians until he had a blinding yet eye-opening encounter with Jesus. Called to become a missionary to the Gentiles, Paul ultimately made three long missionary journeys, starting new churches and revisiting many of them.

Read	Checkpoints
☑ Psalms 38–41	• tongues of fire
☑ Acts 1–3	• a voice from heaven
☑ Acts 4–6	
☑ Acts 7–9	• escape in a basket
☑ Acts 10–12	• an invitation to dine
☑ Acts 13–15	• the first "jailhouse rock"
☑ Acts 16–18	

The word of God hidden in the heart is a stubborn voice to suppress.

—Billy Graham

Share the Journey

How did you experience God's heart in this week's reading?

Something you learned or an insight you gained

A verse or passage you'd like to remember

Questions

God on the move

Paul's third journey to preach the gospel, start new churches, and encourage believers begins in chapter 19 of Acts. The next chapter lists Paul's companions—including Luke—on most of his journey. From chapter 20 through the end of the book, Luke occasionally uses the pronoun *we*, making it clear he's writing an eyewitness account.

Paul's conviction and firm hope in Jesus' resurrection riled both Jews and Gentiles. Rioting and unrest eventually sent Paul to prison—although he had done nothing wrong—but also gave him opportunities to preach to Roman rulers. Paul appealed his case to Caesar and, after surviving a shipwreck, finally arrived in Rome.

The fast-paced book of Joshua begins a section of the Old Testament known as the books of history. The events in Joshua span about ten years. Joshua led the Israelites across the Jordan River as God, faithful to his promises, took the Israelites into the Promised Land to claim it as their own. After following God's commands and achieving victories at Jericho and Ai, the people renewed their covenant with God at Mount Ebal as Moses had instructed them to do.

Read	Checkpoints
☑ Acts 19–21	• seven sons
☑ Acts 22–24	• a poisonous snakebite
☑ Acts 25–28	• two sets of twelve stones
☑ Joshua 1–3	• buried treasure
☑ Joshua 4–6	• thirty-one kings
☑ Joshua 7–9	
☑ Joshua 10–12	

The longer you read the Bible, the more you will like it; it will grow sweeter and sweeter.

—*William Romaine*

Share the Journey

How did you experience God's heart in this week's reading?

Something you learned or an insight you gained

A verse or passage you'd like to remember

Questions

by grace
through faith

The Israelites' conquest of the Promised Land didn't happen all at once. God listed for Joshua the land Israel had yet to possess, and then God himself drove out the inhabitants of those areas because of Joshua's age. Chapters 14 through 19 of the book of Joshua detail the distribution among Israel's tribes of all the land west of the Jordan River.

The book of Romans introduces a section of the New Testament comprised of letters written to churches and individuals, primarily by some of the apostles, the disciples closest to Jesus who later led the fledgling church. The apostle Paul, who wrote Romans, was the exception—he had persecuted the church until Jesus appeared to him on the road to Damascus (Acts 9).

When Paul wrote this letter, he had not yet been to Rome. The church in Rome had both Jewish and Gentile believers, with different backgrounds that sometimes caused problems. Paul wrote to instruct them about essentials of the gospel and their need to live in harmony. His central theme throughout the letter is salvation for both Jews and Gentiles by grace through faith.

Read	Checkpoints
☑ Joshua 13–15	• cities of refuge
☑ Joshua 16–18	• buried bones
☑ Joshua 19–21	• truth exchanged for a lie
☑ Joshua 22–24	• a demonstration of God's love
☑ Romans 1–3	• no condemnation
☑ Romans 4–6	
☑ Romans 7–9	

The Bible is still to me the lovely and beloved book. That in itself is enough to get me out of bed in the morning!

—Alec Motyer

Share the Journey

How did you experience God's heart in this week's reading?

Something you learned or an insight you gained

A verse or passage you'd like to remember

Questions

disobedience
and rescue

Paul finished his letter to the Christians in Rome with a discussion of God's plan for the Israelites (the Jews) who had rejected Jesus and how believers should regard them. The final chapters of the letter provide specific instructions and encouragement for living as Christians, individually and as a church.

The book of Judges covers the years between Israel's settlement of the Promised Land and the reigns of the nation's first kings. During these years, the people continued a spiral of disobedience to God that had begun even before the death of Joshua. They failed to completely drive out the Canaanites from the land and instead intermarried with them and even worshiped the Canaanite gods.

The Israelites' disobedience always led to suffering at the hands of foreign peoples. Whenever the Israelites finally called out to God for help, he raised up leaders known as judges, who rescued and then ruled various tribes at different times. Chapters 3 through 16 tell the stories of twelve of the judges in chronological order. But the nation's downward cycle continued.

Read	Checkpoints
☑ Romans 10–12	• a living sacrifice
☑ Romans 13–16	• burden bearing
☑ Judges 1–3	• two brave women
☑ Judges 4–6	
☑ Judges 7–9	• a piece of fleece
☑ Judges 10–12	• an unwise vow
☑ Judges 13–16	

Your relationship with God will never be any stronger, it will never be any more vibrant, and it will never be any more genuine than your relationship with the Word of God.

—Nancy Leigh DeMoss

Share the Journey

How did you experience God's heart in this week's reading?

Something you learned or an insight you gained

A verse or passage you'd like to remember

Questions

01/16

darkness and light

The final five chapters of Judges depart from a chronological presentation. The distressing events recounted there are presented out of order to emphasize the great spiritual decline the nation of Israel experienced during the era of the judges.

The book of Ruth tells a completely different kind of story from those years, however. Ruth, a young Moabite widow, chose to be a follower of the God of Israel. As a result of Ruth's faithfulness, God not only provided food and shelter for Ruth and her mother-in-law but also a husband for Ruth. Boaz and Ruth had a son who became the grandfather of Israel's great King David. The themes of loyal love and redemption, so strong in Ruth's story, also illustrate the loyal love and the redemption plan of God himself.

The apostle Paul wrote the letter of 1 Corinthians to the Christians in the Greek city of Corinth, notorious for its immorality. Paul's letter is a response to information he had received from leaders and others in the church there, which Paul had started on his second missionary journey. The young congregation needed to get back on track and deal with issues of disunity and sexual immorality.

Read	Checkpoints
☑ Judges 17–19	• war with Benjamin's tribe
☑ Judges 20–21	• two Moabite widows
☑ Ruth 1–4	
☑ 1 Corinthians 1–2	• a helpful relative
☑ 1 Corinthians 3–4	• planting and watering
☑ 1 Corinthians 5–6	
☑ 1 Corinthians 7–9	• running for a crown

Unless we form the habit of going to the Bible in bright moments as well as in trouble, we cannot fully respond to its consolation because we lack equilibrium between light and darkness.

—Helen Keller

Share the Journey

How did you experience God's heart in this week's reading?

Something you learned or an insight you gained

A verse or passage you'd like to remember

Questions

01/23

give us a king!

In the concluding chapters of 1 Corinthians, we find instructions about worship, the Lord's Supper, and spiritual gifts. Chapter 13 forms a famous passage often called the love chapter of the Bible, and chapter 15 provides a clear presentation of the gospel Paul preached and the significance of the resurrection.

Near the end of the era of Israel's judges, Samuel led Israel as both prophet (one who speaks for God) and judge. The book of 1 Samuel recounts his early years and his military victories over the Philistines, then turns to focus on the rise and fall of Saul, Israel's first king. Despite warnings, the Israelites had asked for a king like those of the nations around them, and God honored their demand, but Saul's refusal to follow God faithfully led to a tragic reign.

Samuel delivered the news that God had taken the kingdom from Saul, and after returning home Samuel did not go to see Saul again. Although God had rejected Saul as a consequence of his disobedience, Saul would remain in power until his death.

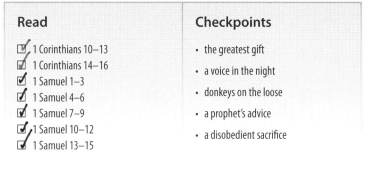

Read	Checkpoints
☑ 1 Corinthians 10–13	• the greatest gift
☑ 1 Corinthians 14–16	• a voice in the night
☑ 1 Samuel 1–3	• donkeys on the loose
☑ 1 Samuel 4–6	• a prophet's advice
☑ 1 Samuel 7–9	• a disobedient sacrifice
☑ 1 Samuel 10–12	
☑ 1 Samuel 13–15	

To what greater inspiration and counsel can we turn than to the imperishable truth to be found in this treasure house, the Bible?

—*Queen Elizabeth II*

Share the Journey

How did you experience God's heart in this week's reading?

Something you learned or an insight you gained

A verse or passage you'd like to remember

Questions

01/30

chosen by God

God sent Samuel to anoint David with oil, setting him apart to become king. A young shepherd-musician from Bethlehem, David had strong faith in God that soon showed itself in combat with Goliath, the Philistine giant. David served in King Saul's court, but eventually Saul's jealousy forced David to flee.

The second half of 1 Samuel chronicles David's life as a fugitive in the wilderness and in enemy territory plus Saul's continuing, willful disobedience of God's commands. David refused to kill Saul despite opportunities to do so, and Saul eventually committed suicide in battle. The path was finally clear for David to be king.

Paul followed up his first letter to the Christians in Corinth with the letter known as 2 Corinthians. This time he emphasized his own authority as an apostle in order to counter charges from false teachers who had stirred up the young Corinthian church against him. Despite the personal nature of the situation, however, Paul used it as an occasion to continue imparting foundational teachings of Christian faith and ministry. The many important doctrines he touched on could help the church in Corinth solve its problems.

Read	Checkpoints
☑ 1 Samuel 16–18	• a king's armor
☑ 1 Samuel 19–21	• murdered priests
☑ 1 Samuel 22–24	
☑ 1 Samuel 25–27	• a wise, tactful wife
☑ 1 Samuel 28–31	• a meeting with a medium
☑ 2 Corinthians 1–3	• a time for judgment
☑ 2 Corinthians 4–6	

You can learn more about human nature by reading the Bible than by living in New York.

—*William Lyon Phelps*

Share the Journey

How did you experience God's heart in this week's reading?

Something you learned or an insight you gained

A verse or passage you'd like to remember

Questions

02/06

a man after God's own heart

Paul's second letter to the Corinthians continues with instruction about Christian living and evidence of Paul's integrity and authority as an apostle. Paul also covers true repentance, giving, and spiritual warfare before contrasting his own service with that of the false teachers who were maligning him.

David's story continues in 2 Samuel. David reigned from Hebron over the tribe of Judah, but the rest of Israel remained loyal to Saul's son Ishbosheth. The early chapters of the book detail the fighting between the forces of Ishbosheth and David. After two of his own captains murdered Ishbosheth, the elders of Israel anointed David king over all Israel.

David desired to build a temple for God in Jerusalem, but God said no. God promised David, however, that one of David's descendants would reign forever. David proved that he was indeed a man after God's own heart (1 Samuel 13:14) when the prophet Nathan confronted him about his sin with Bathsheba and the murder of her husband, Uriah. The consequences within David's family would be long lasting, however, and eventually put David on the run once again, his kingship under attack by his son Absalom.

Read

- ☑ 2 Corinthians 7–9
- ☑ 2 Corinthians 10–13
- ☑ 2 Samuel 1–3
- ☑ 2 Samuel 4–6
- ☑ 2 Samuel 7–9
- ☑ 2 Samuel 10–12
- ☑ 2 Samuel 13–15

Checkpoints

- cheerful giving
- a thorn in the flesh
- the ark in Jerusalem
- a king's kindness
- a poor man's lamb

Let us never forget that the message of the Bible is addressed primarily to the mind, to the understanding.

—D. Martyn Lloyd-Jones

Share the Journey

How did you experience God's heart in this week's reading?

Something you learned or an insight you gained

A verse or passage you'd like to remember

Questions

02/13

walk wisely

David's son Absalom listened to the wrong advice and was killed by David's commander, Joab. Despite his son's treason, David greatly mourned Absalom's death, even as he returned to Jerusalem to reestablish his reign. Chapter 22, a psalm (see Psalm 18), expresses David's strong faith throughout his lifetime. The last four chapters of 2 Samuel are not placed chronologically.

Paul's letter to the Galatians (Galatia was a region in what is now Turkey) countered the false teaching that salvation depends on keeping the Jewish law. Paul emphasizes repeatedly in this letter that the truth of the gospel is salvation through faith in Jesus alone. He encourages and instructs believers to rely on the Holy Spirit's power and guidance in order to live in freedom and love.

The book of 1 Kings continues the story of the nation of Israel. Before he died, David had announced that God had chosen his son Solomon to be the next king and to build the temple (1 Chronicles 28:5–6). When Solomon began his reign by asking God for wisdom, God gave him not only great wisdom but great wealth and honor too.

Read	Checkpoints
☑ 2 Samuel 16–18	• tangled in a tree
☑ 2 Samuel 19–21	• a thousand sacrifices
☑ 2 Samuel 22–24	• two mothers
☐ Galatians 1–3	• the cedars of Lebanon
☐ Galatians 4–6	• the fruit of the Spirit
☐ 1 Kings 1–3	
☐ 1 Kings 4–6	

This is why He speaks [in the Bible]—to cause us to encounter him in a way that we otherwise might not have the privilege of seeing or being a part of.

—Priscilla Shirer

Share the Journey

How did you experience God's heart in this week's reading?

Something you learned or an insight you gained

A verse or passage you'd like to remember

Questions

02/20

division and unity

To protect his people, God had commanded that they not marry foreigners and that the king should not have many wives. But Solomon chose not to obey God in these matters, and toward the end of his reign the impact of his decisions could be seen. Solomon compromised his faith and joined his foreign wives in worshiping their gods. God told him that as a result the nation of Israel ultimately would split apart.

The tribes of Judah and Benjamin remained with Solomon's successors and became known as the southern kingdom (Judah). The remaining ten tribes rebelled against Solomon's son Rehoboam over their heavy taxes and forced labor and became known as the northern kingdom (Israel). Jeroboam soon led Israel into idol worship. Despite warnings by God's prophets and the efforts of some good kings in Judah, the people of the divided kingdom moved farther and farther away from obeying God.

Paul's letter to the Christians in Ephesus (near the Aegean Sea) focuses on the spiritual blessings given to all believers, the unity of all who believe—the body of Christ—and the behaviors and responsibilities those blessings and that unity require.

Read

☑ 1 Kings 7–9
☑ 1 Kings 10–12
☑ 1 Kings 13–15
☑ 1 Kings 16–18
☑ 1 Kings 19–22
☑ Ephesians 1–3
☐ Ephesians 4–6

Checkpoints

• two golden calves

• bulls and Baal

• a tired prophet

• the Chief Cornerstone

• spiritual armor

When all your favorite preachers are gone, and all their books forgotten, you will have your Bible. Master it. Master it.

—John Piper

Share the Journey

How did you experience God's heart in this week's reading?

Something you learned or an insight you gained

A verse or passage you'd like to remember

Questions

02/27

disobedience, decline, and disaster

The Israelites' idol worship and unwillingness to repent led God to punish and discipline his people as he had warned. Samaria, the capital of the northern kingdom, fell to the Assyrians in 722 BC after a three-year siege, and most of the people of Israel went as captives to Assyria. More than a century later, after Babylon had conquered the Assyrians, the southern kingdom ended in 586 BC when Nebuchadnezzar destroyed the capital city of Jerusalem. Some of Judah's citizens had been taken to Babylon earlier; most of the Jews remaining now joined them as captives. Their exile in Babylon would last seventy years.

Second Kings records these sad events along with the chaos and decline that preceded them. Reading this book can feel like a roller-coaster ride gone bad as God's prophets call the kings and people back to God but few listen or respond.

Despite Judah's fall, God would remain true to his promise to the line of David. King Jehoiachin, imprisoned in Babylon before Jerusalem fell, was released from prison after thirty-seven years. This kindness extended to Jehoiachin ends 2 Kings on a note of hope.

Read	Checkpoints
☑ 2 Kings 1–3	• a chariot of fire
☑ 2 Kings 4–7	• seven dips in the Jordan
☐ 2 Kings 8–10	• a floating ax head
☑ 2 Kings 11–14	• a feast for wild dogs
☑ 2 Kings 15–17	• a lost-and-found book
☑ 2 Kings 18–21	
☑ 2 Kings 22–25	

Never let good books take the place of the Bible. Drink from the Well, not from the streams that flow from the Well.

—Amy Carmichael

Share the Journey

How did you experience God's heart in this week's reading?

Something you learned or an insight you gained

A verse or passage you'd like to remember

Questions

79

03/06

peace and praise

The church at Philippi, a city in Macedonia (now Greece), was greatly diverse in racial ethnicity and social rank. Paul commended their love and joy and encouraged them to make Jesus their focus and Jesus' life of humble service their pattern. He thanked them for partnering with him in his work by their gifts, and he shared the secret of contentment. Paul wrote this letter to the Philippians from prison, possibly in Rome.

Part 2 of the book of Psalms (Psalms 42–72) probably was compiled and added during King Solomon's reign. Some of these psalms make specific references to David's life. Perhaps most well known is Psalm 51, written after David repented of his sin with Bathsheba. Some others are imprecatory psalms, expressing strong negative emotion toward enemies and those set against God, helping us comprehend God's view of evil.

Hebrew poetry did not rely on rhyme but on parallelism, the way thoughts are arranged. A second line might repeat the thought of the preceding line or offer a contrast. Sometimes the second and succeeding lines build upon the thought of the first line. These basic forms also mix to form more complex patterns.

Read	Checkpoints
☑ Philippians 1–4	• shining lights
☑ Psalms 42–45	• a righteous judge
☑ Psalms 46–49	• a fool's heart
☑ Psalms 50–53	• a strong tower
☑ Psalms 54–57	• a parched, weary land
☑ Psalms 58–61	
☑ Psalms 62–66	

Read the Bible in a commonsense way. . . . Get into an easy chair: read it comfortably. . . . Do not make a penance of what ought to be a pleasure.

—Charles Spurgeon

 **Share the Journey**

How did you experience God's heart in this week's reading?

Something you learned or an insight you gained

A verse or passage you'd like to remember

Questions

81

03|13

remember the past

The second part of the book of Psalms closes with the psalms in this week's reading. Psalm 70 and 71, which are psalms of lament, ask intently for God's help. Psalm 72, written by Solomon, is a royal psalm, praising the Messiah who would come to reign over the earth.

First Chronicles served the Jewish people as a refresher course on faith. After seventy years of exile, a remnant of several thousand Jews returned to Judah from Babylon. But their early strong dedication to rebuilding the temple faded, and they turned away from following God. First Chronicles reviews their religious history from creation through King David's reign. It emphasizes the obedience needed if the nation wanted to experience God's blessing. The first nine chapters present a variety of genealogies, recalling that God worked with his chosen people from the beginning. The remainder of the book focuses on David and the national well-being that resulted from David's commitment to following God.

Ezra, a priest and scribe who compiled the book, incorporated information from 1 and 2 Samuel and 1 and 2 Kings. He mentions other sources, not part of Scripture, as well.

Read	Checkpoints
☑ Psalms 67–69	• kings bringing presents
☑ Psalms 70–72	• David's sisters
☑ 1 Chronicles 1–3	• 212 gatekeepers
☑ 1 Chronicles 4–6	• water from Bethlehem's well
☑ 1 Chronicles 7–9	• the ark on a cart
☑ 1 Chronicles 10–12	
☑ 1 Chronicles 13–15	

The best way I've found to start hearing the Lord's whispers in my heart is by getting into his Word and letting his Word get into me.

—*Lysa TerKeurst*

Share the Journey

How did you experience God's heart in this week's reading?

Something you learned or an insight you gained

A verse or passage you'd like to remember

Questions

83

exalted over all

The second half of 1 Chronicles continues the story of Israel's faith history. The ark returned to Jerusalem, David's military efforts brought peace, and David made plans and preparations for building the temple. The book concludes when the nation's worship of God was well established and Solomon had been anointed king.

Colossians, in the New Testament, is another letter written by Paul from prison in Rome, this time to the church in Colossae, a hundred miles east of Ephesus. Paul wrote to correct the wrong teaching that Gentile Christians must adhere to the Jewish law, but even more he wrote to correct other false doctrines creeping into the church from Greek influence. The letter focuses on who Jesus is—his position over creation and his power over all other powers—and what Christian spirituality is and is not.

Like 1 Chronicles, the second book of Chronicles looks back at the religious life of the nation of Israel in order to encourage and instruct the Jews who had returned from exile. After Solomon began to reign, he asked God to help him rule with wisdom and began to build the long-awaited and glorious temple of God.

Read	Checkpoints
☐ 1 Chronicles 16–18	• an angel's drawn sword
☐ 1 Chronicles 19–22	• the hope of glory
☐ 1 Chronicles 23–26	• handwritten by Paul
☐ 1 Chronicles 27–29	• the veil
☐ Colossians 1–4	• cymbals, harps, and trumpets
☐ 2 Chronicles 1–3	
☐ 2 Chronicles 4–6	

May we as women be filled with the Word so we may teach and exhort with all wisdom.

—Sandra Glahn

Share the Journey

How did you experience God's heart in this week's reading?

Something you learned or an insight you gained

A verse or passage you'd like to remember

Questions

03/27

good kings, bad kings

Second Chronicles outlines the reigns of Solomon and the kings who followed him in Judah. The rulers who followed God, obeyed his laws, and led the people to do the same brought blessing to the nation. Those who worshiped idols—false gods— and even promoted idol worship led the nation away from God.

Solomon reigned for forty years, amassing vast wealth and military might. When Solomon died, his son Rehoboam succeeded him. Within a short time, the northern tribes rebelled, and the nation of Israel split in two. Only the tribes of Judah and Benjamin remained under Rehoboam's rule in the south. The remaining tribes formed the northern kingdom of Israel under Jeroboam, who set up his own idols for the people to worship and appointed his own priests.

The Levites and priests throughout the northern kingdom and many Israelites who remained faithful to God then moved to Judah. From that point 2 Chronicles remains focused on the rulers of the southern kingdom—an up-and-down parade of wicked and godly kings and their rebellion and reforms.

Read	Checkpoints
☑ 2 Chronicles 7–9 ☑ 2 Chronicles 10–12 ☑ 2 Chronicles 13–15 ☑ 2 Chronicles 16–18 ☑ 2 Chronicles 19–21 ☑ 2 Chronicles 22–24 ☑ 2 Chronicles 25–27	• glory in the temple • monkeys on merchant ships • a severe foot disease • sheep without a shepherd • a letter from Elijah

When you read God's Word, you must constantly be saying to yourself, "It is talking to me, and about me."

—Søren Kierkegaard

Share the Journey

How did you experience God's heart in this week's reading?

Something you learned or an insight you gained

A verse or passage you'd like to remember

Questions

04/03

return and rebuilding

Despite the reforms of Hezekiah and Josiah, the hearts and practices of the people of Judah remained far from God. As the prophets had warned, destruction and exile resulted. But God remained faithful, as he always had. Babylon fell to Persia in 539 BC, and 2 Chronicles ends with a proclamation by King Cyrus of Persia, releasing the Jews to return home to rebuild the temple.

Paul's letters to the church at Thessalonica, in Greece, encouraged the young congregation to stand firm despite opposition and persecution. Paul had started this church but had not been able to spend much time there (Acts 17). Paul delivers a lot of teaching on many topics in these short letters, including details about Jesus' second coming.

The book of Ezra documents the return of the exiles to Judah, the rebuilding and dedication of the temple in 515 BC, and the reforms Ezra instituted when he arrived about sixty years later. Zerubbabel, the grandson of King Jehoiachin, led the first returning exiles back to Judah and began rebuilding the temple despite interference from people living in the land.

Read

- ☑ 2 Chronicles 28–30
- ☑ 2 Chronicles 31–33
- ☑ 2 Chronicles 34–36
- ☑ 1 Thessalonians 1–5
- ☑ 2 Thessalonians 1–3
- ☑ Ezra 1–3
- ☑ Ezra 4–6

Checkpoints

- a closed temple
- a thief in the night
- the lawless one
- a search of the archives
- a joyful Passover

The existence of the Bible, as a book for the people, is the greatest benefit the human race has ever experienced. Every attempt to belittle it is a crime against humanity.

—*Immanuel Kant*

Share the Journey

How did you experience God's heart in this week's reading?

Something you learned or an insight you gained

A verse or passage you'd like to remember

Questions

04/10

for such a time
as this

Led first by Zerubbabel, then by Ezra, and then by Nehemiah (a
Jew born in exile who became cupbearer to King Artaxerxes),
the Jews rebuilt the temple and the walls of Jerusalem. They
overcame opposition, resettled in the city and surrounding area,
and began to observe the law given to Moses once again. Nehemiah served as governor. But despite the blessings of this new
start, the people succumbed to some of the same sins that led
to the fall of Jerusalem years earlier, including intermarrying
with foreign women, disregarding the Sabbath, and allowing
compromises within the priesthood.

Not all the Jews returned to Judah immediately after the
exile. Esther's story of intrigue, trust, and courage occurred
before either Ezra or Nehemiah traveled to Jerusalem. The book
might have been written by Esther's relative Mordecai. God is
not mentioned in the account, but he is clearly present. Despite
how cut off from God the exiles must have felt, God remained
sovereign and true to his promises. Those who came against his
people would be brought down; God would faithfully protect
his people, even in a foreign land.

Read	Checkpoints
☑ Ezra 7–10	• a letter from a king
☑ Nehemiah 1–3	• a nighttime scouting mission
☑ Nehemiah 4–6	
☑ Nehemiah 7–9	• beard hairs
☑ Nehemiah 10–13	• a dethroned queen
☑ Esther 1–3	
☑ Esther 4–6	• a golden scepter

Scripture changes us at the cellular level. It touches our hearts, renews our minds, and ultimately transforms our behavior.

—*Liz Curtis Higgs*

Share the Journey

How did you experience God's heart in this week's reading?

Something you learned or an insight you gained

A verse or passage you'd like to remember

Questions

91

04|17

answers and
questions

Esther implored King Xerxes to save the Jews in Persia. He decreed that they would be allowed to kill anyone who might attack them. The thanksgiving feast Purim got its name from the Babylonian word meaning "to cast lots" (*pur*), as Haman had done.

The books of 1 and 2 Timothy are letters from the apostle Paul to a beloved young minister. Timothy traveled with Paul on his second missionary journey. Later, after a visit to Ephesus, Paul left Timothy in Ephesus to assist the church there. The first letter instructed Timothy about how church members and leaders should function. Paul wrote the second letter knowing the end of his own life was near. He encouraged Timothy to remain committed to Christ, to preaching the gospel, and to teaching the believers.

The book of Job, which explores the existence of suffering, begins a section of the Old Testament known as the books of poetry, or the wisdom books. Although Job might have been written during the time of Solomon, its story took place much earlier, possibly during the time of Abraham.

Read	Checkpoints
☑ Esther 7–10	• a joyful celebration
☑ 1 Timothy 1–3	• prayers for all people
☑ 1 Timothy 4–6	
☑ 2 Timothy 1–4	• a godly mother and grandmother
☑ Job 1–4	• two meetings with God
☑ Job 5–8	
☑ Job 9–12	• a bitter wife

The Bible stands alone as God's only perfect guide to life and growth.

—John Townsend

Share the Journey

How did you experience God's heart in this week's reading?

Something you learned or an insight you gained

A verse or passage you'd like to remember

Questions

93

04/24

conversation and confrontation

After Job suffered his devastating losses, three friends came to comfort him. For seven days and nights, they sat with him silently, but then they began to speak. They all believed God brings misfortune as punishment for sin. Job knew he had lived obediently, but he had no explanation for his circumstances. Job never blamed God for his misfortunes, but he felt betrayed because God would not explain himself.

When Job and his friends reached a stalemate, a younger man, Elihu, entered the conversation. Elihu affirmed that God is just and powerful. He believed that God might use suffering to teach us and give us insight. Elihu confronted Job about making demands of God—an attitude of pride.

God entered the conversation next. Chapters 38–42 present God's questions to Job about his wisdom, power, and rule—questions Job realized he could not answer. Finally understanding that God, who is over all, is not obligated to reward obedience or to explain his actions, Job turned back to serving God. God then restored Job's fortune twice over and blessed him with more children and a long life.

Read	Checkpoints
☑ Job 13–16	• miserable comforters
☑ Job 17–21	• Job's redeemer
☑ Job 22–26	• the whirlwind
☑ Job 27–30	• Leviathan
☑ Job 31–34	• beautiful daughters
☑ Job 35–38	
☑ Job 39–42	

Is the Bible the Word of God? Then let us all resolve from this day forward to prize the Bible more.

—J. C. Ryle

Share the Journey

How did you experience God's heart in this week's reading?

Something you learned or an insight you gained

A verse or passage you'd like to remember

Questions

05/01

songs of trust
and joy

Psalms 73 through 89 form part 3 of the book of Psalms. Most were written by Asaph, a musician among those appointed by King David to lead music during worship at the tabernacle. Like the entire book of Psalms, Asaph's psalms express a range of emotions—lament and trust, despair and praise, pleading and thanksgiving, peace and proclamation—and Asaph writes about his own experiences as well as those of the nation of Israel.

Part 4 of Psalms begins with Psalm 90, written by Moses from the perspective of the Israelite community. He complains about the brevity of life and about God's judgment, all the while acknowledging God's care and provision and praying for a renewed and joyful experience of life with God. Psalm 91 might also have been written by Moses. Verses 9 through 16 address the coming Messiah; during Jesus' testing in the wilderness, Satan tried to use some of these verses against Jesus.

Some of the most inspiring psalms are the royal psalms, such as Psalms 74 and 93. The royal psalms proclaim that God is king over all creation, king over the Israelites, and the king who will come again to judge and rule eternally.

Read	Checkpoints
☑ Psalms 73–76	• words for the next generation
☑ Psalms 77–78	• the Shepherd of Israel
☑ Psalms 79–82	• a transformed valley
☑ Psalms 83–86	• the city of God
☑ Psalms 87–89	• singing trees
☑ Psalms 90–93	
☑ Psalms 94–97	

The amazing thing about the Bible, and especially the psalms, is that it not only presents us with thoughts to think and beliefs to embrace but also with feelings to feel.

—*Nancy Guthrie*

Share the Journey

How did you experience God's heart in this week's reading?

Something you learned or an insight you gained

A verse or passage you'd like to remember

Questions

97

05/08

wise words

The songs that close part 4 of Psalms ring with praise for God's righteousness, holiness, faithfulness, love, mercy, creation, care, and forgiveness.

Titus and Philemon are short letters from the apostle Paul. Titus had traveled with Paul and assisted his work in various ways. When Paul wrote this letter, Titus was ministering with a church on the island of Crete. The letter gives succinct instructions to church leaders, including the importance of teaching God's people to do good works. In his letter to Philemon, a Gentile Christian and a church leader in Colossae, Paul tactfully pleads for the life of Onesimus, a slave owned by Philemon. Onesimus had apparently stolen from Philemon and run away, met Paul, and become a Christian. Although by Roman law Philemon could have had Onesimus executed, Paul asked Philemon to accept Onesimus back as a beloved brother and to free him for service to the church.

The book of Proverbs is part of the poetry section of the Old Testament, which is sometimes called the wisdom books. A proverb is a saying that presents a general truth about life. King Solomon wrote most of the book of Proverbs.

Read	Checkpoints
☑ Psalms 98–102	• God's sheep
☑ Psalms 103–104	• wine, oil, and bread
☑ Psalms 105–106	• a slave now a brother
☑ Titus 1–3, Philemon	• wisdom's house
☑ Proverbs 1–4	• a gold ring in a pig's nose
☑ Proverbs 5–8	
☑ Proverbs 9–12	

I confess how Bible study often works for me. I find a passage that brings comfort, shelter, and encouragement. I memorize and savor it. Then eventually I read the surrounding context and find I have work to do: actions and attitudes to adjust.

—*Nancy Karpenske*

Share the Journey

How did you experience God's heart in this week's reading?

Something you learned or an insight you gained

A verse or passage you'd like to remember

Questions

05/15

where knowledge begins

Written as poetry like the Psalms, the book of Proverbs contains short, memorable observations about wise and foolish living. Except for the first nine chapters and the last two, the book is not arranged by topic, but nearly three dozen subjects—including discipline, friendship, laziness, pride, and speech—occur again and again. The overall theme of Proverbs is that having true knowledge begins with fearing (having awe and respect for) God.

A variety of relationships between the lines characterized Hebrew poetry—statements generally repeat, contrast, compare, or complete one another. Many of the proverbs also use imagery from everyday life to illustrate the principles being taught. Though many of the proverbs read like promises, a proverb is a general statement only; exceptions can exist. But the wisdom in the book of Proverbs has universal application—following the principles in Proverbs will lead anyone in any society to a happier and better life.

The book of Proverbs was expanded during the reign of King Hezekiah (Proverbs 25:1) to include more of King Solomon's thousands of proverbs. Two other writers, Agur and Lemuel, contributed the proverbs in the last two chapters.

Read	Checkpoints
☑ Proverbs 13–15	• a goal achieved
☑ Proverbs 16–17	• a soft answer
☑ Proverbs 18–20	• words like a honeycomb
☑ Proverbs 21–23	• a lazy man and a lion
☑ Proverbs 24–26	• apples of gold
☑ Proverbs 27–29	
☑ Proverbs 30–31	

When we pick up Scripture, we do not read (a verb); we become (a realization).

—Ann Voskamp

Share the Journey

How did you experience God's heart in this week's reading?

Something you learned or an insight you gained

A verse or passage you'd like to remember

Questions

101

05/22

a better way

Just as Jewish Christians struggled with whether Gentile believers needed to follow the Jewish law, they also struggled with whether they themselves could truly have a relationship with God simply through faith in Jesus. In addition, Jews who became Christians faced rejection and economic discrimination within their communities. Who wrote the book of Hebrews isn't known for certain, but the message of the book is clear: Don't go back—you made the right choice. Christ is superior—to angels, to Moses, to the Jewish high priest, to the system of sacrifices, to the old covenant. The old way has ended, the new has come. This would be especially important for Jewish believers to remember when Nero began persecuting Christians in AD 64.

The book of Ecclesiastes might be evidence that King Solomon repented late in life of his idol worship and marrying hundreds of foreign wives, a conclusion not fully seen until the final chapters of the book. Solomon had sought fulfillment in the pursuit of wisdom, pleasure, accomplishment, and possessions, only to discover that life without God had no meaning. His book serves to teach others to avoid repeating his mistakes.

Read	Checkpoints
☑ Hebrews 1–4	• a high priest forever
☑ Hebrews 5–7	• a new covenant
☑ Hebrews 8–10	
☑ Hebrews 11–13	• the great Shepherd
☑ Ecclesiastes 1–3	• eternity in our hearts
☑ Ecclesiastes 4–6	• a cord of three strands
☑ Ecclesiastes 7–9	

Reading the Bible can be like enjoying a good piece of chocolate.

—*Mary Kassian*

Share the Journey

How did you experience God's heart in this week's reading?

Something you learned or an insight you gained

A verse or passage you'd like to remember

Questions

05/29

love, faith, and mercy

The author of Ecclesiastes, King Solomon, also wrote the book known as the Song of Songs, or the Song of Solomon. This love poem about Solomon and his bride from a Galilean village celebrates marriage and sexual love within marriage. The poem tells the story of the couple's first meetings and wedding, their wedding night, and their adjustment to marriage. Presented in a form common in the ancient Middle East, not everything in the book follows a chronological order, and a chorus sometimes interrupts to emphasize, warn, or make a transition.

Jesus' half-brother James likely wrote the book of James, possibly one of the oldest New Testament books. James wrote to Jewish Christians scattered from Jerusalem to deepen their faith when faced with various difficulties in life. Often relying on Jesus' teaching, James provides practical advice for living as people of faith and emphasizes making faith evident by doing good works and controlling what we say.

Isaiah prophesied to God's people about events during his own lifetime and in the future. Chapters 1–39 relate to the years leading up to the Assyrian invasion. The remaining chapters speak of the exile in Babylon and the return to Judah as well as the coming of the Savior.

Read	Checkpoints
☑ Ecclesiastes 10–12	• little foxes
☑ Song of Solomon 1–2	• a seal upon the heart
☑ Song of Solomon 3–5	
☑ Song of Solomon 6–8	• a face in a mirror
☑ James 1–5	• a great forest fire
☑ Isaiah 1–3	• a vision of God
☑ Isaiah 4–7	

The Bible is my oxygen. . . . How could I live a single day in this world of illusion without God's inerrant Word?

—Ray Ortlund

Share the Journey

How did you experience God's heart in this week's reading?

Something you learned or an insight you gained

A verse or passage you'd like to remember

Questions

06/05

sorrow and salvation

The book of Isaiah begins a section of the Old Testament containing the messages of the prophets. With the exception of Lamentations, the first five books of prophecy are long and for that reason are sometimes called the major prophets.

Isaiah lived in Jerusalem, was married, and had two sons. He spoke for God for nearly sixty years, beginning in 740 BC. Tradition says that Isaiah was martyred by being sawn in two.

Most of the book of Isaiah is poetry, and like the wisdom books, the poetry of Isaiah utilizes comparison and contrast plus symbolic visual images. The prophecies themselves are not always chronological, and a single prophecy can have more than one fulfillment.

Isaiah prophesied primarily to Judah but also to Israel. Destruction would soon fall on the entire nation as God used first Assyria and later Babylon to discipline his people. Chapters 1 through 39 focus on the futility of not turning to God for help and on God's righteous judgment of all the nations. Yet numerous prophecies of the coming Savior also are found in the first half of Isaiah.

Read	Checkpoints
☑ Isaiah 8–10	• the Prince of Peace
☑ Isaiah 11–13	• a rod and a branch
☑ Isaiah 14–17	
☑ Isaiah 18–21	• a wolf and a lamb
☑ Isaiah 22–25	• a sure foundation
☑ Isaiah 26–28	• the potter and the clay
☑ Isaiah 29–30	

Trust is the lesson. Jesus loves me, this I know—not because he does just what I'd like, but because the Bible tells me so.

—Elisabeth Elliot

Share the Journey

How did you experience God's heart in this week's reading?

Something you learned or an insight you gained

A verse or passage you'd like to remember

Questions

de\12

a light to the Gentiles

King Hezekiah of Judah is the main character of chapters 36 through 39, which end the first section of Isaiah. Assyria had swept away the northern kingdom and eventually turned on Judah because Hezekiah withheld tribute payments. Hezekiah's response to the situation allowed the Lord to show him mercy and defeat the Assyrian army.

Chapter 40 takes this book of prophecy in a new direction. Up to this point, the focus has been God's righteousness, holiness, and justice. Now the prophet begins to emphasize God's glory, compassion, and grace. God will restore his ruined, exiled people; he will not forget them. A remnant from Judah will return to rebuild the temple at Jerusalem, released from exile by King Cyrus of Persia at God's prompting.

In addition, God would provide salvation to all people through Jesus, introduced as God's servant in chapter 42. He also appears in other chapters in this section, where he is described as the one sent by God and the Spirit, a light to the Gentiles, and the servant of rulers whom kings and princes will worship.

Read	Checkpoints
✓ Isaiah 31–33	• streams in the desert
✓ Isaiah 34–36	• a shadow on the sundial
✓ Isaiah 37–39	
✓ Isaiah 40–42	• wings like eagles
✓ Isaiah 43–45	• the servant of God
✓ Isaiah 46–48	• God the Rock
✓ Isaiah 49–51	

Our Bible was the center of an ever-widening circle of help and hope. Like waifs clustered around a blazing fire, we gathered about it, holding out our hearts to its warmth and light.

—*Corrie ten Boom*

Share the Journey

How did you experience God's heart in this week's reading?

Something you learned or an insight you gained

A verse or passage you'd like to remember

Questions

06/19

stand firm

Beginning at the end of chapter 52 and throughout chapter 53, Isaiah provides another look at the servant to come, Jesus—this time as the suffering servant who takes on the punishment for the sins of all people. Chapter 61 contains the verses Jesus read aloud in the synagogue of Nazareth (Luke 4:16–21) when he began his three-year public ministry.

In chapters 40 through 55, Isaiah's prophecies address those who would be exiled and feel forgotten. The final ten chapters focus on encouraging the Jews who returned to Judah after the exile. A Messiah was coming, and the Gentiles would join the Jews to serve God in a new nation. Despite this hope, the book ends with a final warning about judgment.

The apostle Peter wrote his letters to the early Christians scattered throughout Asia Minor (now Turkey) sometime between the years AD 62 and 67, which led up to his own martyr's death. These believers faced persecution within their communities, and Peter wrote to help them understand, accept, and stand firm through their suffering based on Jesus' own example, and to warn them against false teachings.

Read	Checkpoints
☑ Isaiah 52–54	• a tender plant
☑ Isaiah 55–57	• God's chosen fast
☑ Isaiah 58–60	• new heavens and a new earth
☑ Isaiah 61–63	• royal priests
☑ Isaiah 64–66	• the day of the Lord
☑ 1 Peter 1–5	
☑ 2 Peter 1–3	

The Bible grows more beautiful, as we grow in our understanding of it.

—Johann Wolfgang von Goethe

Share the Journey

How did you experience God's heart in this week's reading?

Something you learned or an insight you gained

A verse or passage you'd like to remember

Questions

a broken covenant

Jeremiah prophesied to the people of Judah during the forty years leading up to the destruction of Jerusalem. Deeply committed to God and his Word, Jeremiah suffered greatly throughout his ministry as the people and leaders of Judah spurned his messages. For this reason Jeremiah has been called the weeping prophet.

Near the start of the sixth century BC, Assyria turned its attention away from Judah for a time, and King Josiah led a revival among God's people. But Babylon crushed Assyria and came against Judah. Jeremiah announced that Babylon was God's chosen instrument to punish his people for their long years of idolatry, and he urged submission to Babylon to avoid utter destruction. Instead the people viewed Jeremiah as a traitor.

God told Jeremiah to use a number of different items—an almond branch, a boiling pot, a linen belt, containers of wine, a pottery jar, and others—as symbolic object lessons. The people's ruinous course remained unchanged, however, no matter how much they were warned about the multitude of ways they had broken their covenant with God. Jeremiah found himself beaten, placed in stocks, and ridiculed.

Read	Checkpoints
☑ Jeremiah 1–3	• an almond branch and a boiling pot
☑ Jeremiah 4–6 (5)	• good and ancient paths
☑ Jeremiah 7–9 (8)	• a linen sash
☑ Jeremiah 10–12	• the potter's house
☑ Jeremiah 13–15	• a broken jar
☑ Jeremiah 16–18	
☑ Jeremiah 19–21	

Everyone is looking for power in a program, in a methodology, in a technique, in anything and everything but that in which God has placed it—his Word.

—R. C. Sproul

Share the Journey

How did you experience God's heart in this week's reading?

Something you learned or an insight you gained

A verse or passage you'd like to remember

Questions

July 3rd (Mikki)

despair and faithfulness

Jeremiah lived in perilous times and often found himself in perilous situations—even at the bottom of a muddy cistern, waiting to die.

For a few years before Babylon came against Judah, Egypt's Pharaoh Necho ruled Judah through King Jehoiakim. The people of Judah turned not to God but to idols and false gods for help. In 605 BC, Nebuchadnezzar of Babylon defeated Necho. Jehoiakim submitted to Nebuchadnezzar, but three years later he rebelled and was deposed. The next king, Jehoiachin, was exiled to Babylon along with many Jewish leaders in 597 BC. Nebuchadnezzar then appointed Zedekiah king of Judah.

Zedekiah disdained both God and Jeremiah's messages from God. But when Nebuchadnezzar won his siege against Jerusalem in 586 BC, he ordered Jeremiah protected and ultimately released, and Jeremiah returned from Ramah to Judah under Gedaliah, the governor Nebuchadnezzar appointed.

Although sometimes despairing, Jeremiah faithfully proclaimed God's messages about the fall of Jerusalem, the exile, and judgment of the nations after God dealt with his own people. But Jeremiah also spoke about future restoration and God's promise of a new covenant to come.

Read	Checkpoints
☑ Jeremiah 22–23 **(23)**	• a branch of righteousness
☑ Jeremiah 24–26	• lying prophets
☑ Jeremiah 27–29	• a letter to captives
☑ Jeremiah 30–31	• an obedient clan
☑ Jeremiah 32–33	• two scrolls
☑ Jeremiah 34–36	
☑ Jeremiah 37–39	

The primary purpose of reading the Bible is not to know the Bible but to know God.

—James Merritt

Share the Journey

How did you experience God's heart in this week's reading?

Something you learned or an insight you gained

A verse or passage you'd like to remember

Questions

07/10

back to Egypt

After most of Judah's citizens went into exile in Babylon, Nebuchadnezzar appointed Gedaliah governor of Judah over the poorest of the people who were left to work the land. Then Gedaliah was assassinated, and the people of Judah wanted to seek safety in Egypt. Although they asked Jeremiah to discover God's will and advise them, they chose not to heed God's command to remain in Judah. Jeremiah was taken against his will into Egypt, where he continued to prophesy against the Jews and other nations. The final chapter of the book of Jeremiah reviews the history of Jerusalem's fall.

Jeremiah is the likely author of the much shorter book of Lamentations, a poetic expression of Jeremiah's deep grief over the ruin of his people. Chapters 1 through 2 and 4 through 5 detail the devastation of Jerusalem. Chapter 3, however, moves from lament to hope to praise to confession. The book ends with a confident prayer; Jeremiah understands that God will not reject his people forever.

The fifth and last part of the book of Psalms opens with a prayer of thanksgiving for deliverance and other psalms of praise.

Read	Checkpoints
☑ Jeremiah 40–43	• ten days
☑ Jeremiah 44–48	• hidden stones
☑ Jeremiah 49–52	• the maker of all
☑ Lamentations 1–2	• the place of honor
☑ Lamentations 3–5	• the order of Melchizedek
☑ Psalms 107–109	
☑ Psalms 110–115	

Down through the years, I turned to the Bible and found in it all that I needed.

—Ruth Bell Graham

Share the Journey

How did you experience God's heart in this week's reading?

Something you learned or an insight you gained

A verse or passage you'd like to remember

Questions

07/17 zoom

sweeter than honey

This week's readings continue in part 5 of the book of Psalms. This final section includes psalms read or sung as part of the Passover celebration (Psalms 113–118; 136), many psalms of thanksgiving and praise, and the longest psalm, Psalm 119, a celebration of God's law and his goodness in revealing it to us.

The Hebrew word *torah*, translated as "law," refers to both the first five books of the Old Testament as well as more generally to all of God's instructions given from Moses through the prophets. *Word* is a general term for all that God has told us. Psalm 119 uses both *law* and *word* to describe God's revelation, as well as *testimonies*, *way*, *precepts*, *statutes*, *commandments*, and *judgments*, and each of these appears multiple times. The psalm also describes the numerous benefits and blessings of following God's law, including peace, joy, strength, freedom, hope, comfort, the power to resist sin, and a thankful heart.

Psalm 119 is an acrostic, with each letter of the Hebrew alphabet having eight verses beginning with that letter—a technique that would have aided memorization.

Read	Checkpoints
☑ Psalms 116–118	• a lamp and a light
☑ Psalm 119:1–88	• seed for sowing
☑ Psalm 119:89–176	
☑ Psalms 120–127	• a mother and child
☑ Psalms 128–134	• man-made gods
☑ Psalms 135–138	• a book of days
☑ Psalms 139–142	

Most of the verses written about praise in God's Word were voiced by people faced with crushing heartaches, injustice, treachery, slander, and scores of other difficult situations.

—Joni Erickson Tada

Share the Journey

How did you experience God's heart in this week's reading?

Something you learned or an insight you gained

A verse or passage you'd like to remember

Questions

119

07/24

visions, judgment, and hope

The final chapters of Psalms ring with praise like the loud and fitting conclusion of a glorious symphony.

Ezekiel, the son of a priest in Judah, was taken to Babylon in 597 BC along with other young leaders of Israel's aristocracy. From Babylon he prophesied to the people of Judah prior to the fall of Jerusalem and later to the exiles in Babylon. Ezekiel was a contemporary of Jeremiah, and like Jeremiah, Ezekiel warned of impending destruction and called out the nation for the actions that made such judgment inevitable. After Jerusalem's fall in 586 BC, Ezekiel's message contained reasons for the exiles to hope.

The first three chapters of Ezekiel tell of his call as a prophet. Chapters 4 through 24 focus on God's judgment of Judah, and chapters 25 through 35 primarily predict God's judgments on his people's enemies. The remaining chapters of the book focus on restoration, including Ezekiel's famous vision of a valley of dry bones coming back to life. Many of Ezekiel's prophecies contain visions as well as symbolic actions, making this book both interesting and challenging for us to read and understand.

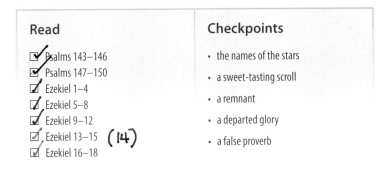

Read	Checkpoints
☑ Psalms 143–146	• the names of the stars
☑ Psalms 147–150	• a sweet-tasting scroll
☑ Ezekiel 1–4	• a remnant
☑ Ezekiel 5–8	• a departed glory
☑ Ezekiel 9–12	• a false proverb
☑ Ezekiel 13–15 **(14)**	
☑ Ezekiel 16–18	

The highest earthly enjoyments are but a shadow of the joy I find in reading God's Word.

—Lady Jane Grey

Share the Journey

How did you experience God's heart in this week's reading?

Something you learned or an insight you gained

A verse or passage you'd like to remember

Questions

121

07/31/2007

the One who is always present

Although God would punish his people, ultimately he would punish their enemies as well. Through Ezekiel, God warned the nations and people of Ammon, Moab, Edom, Philistia, Tyre, and Egypt of circumstances to come and also proclaimed the defeat of Gog and Magog in a future, intense battle. Like the Israelites, other nations also would learn through God's judgments that God is sovereign and in control. He is the LORD, *Yahweh*, "the one who is always present"—an assertion God makes about himself through Ezekiel more than fifty times.

God held the shepherds of Israel, the nation's leaders, responsible both for their wrongdoing and their refusal to do what was right. But Ezekiel also makes clear that individuals are responsible for their own actions and are judged accordingly.

Ezekiel also proclaimed future hope for restoration, with clear references to a united kingdom of God's people, ruled by one king as a good shepherd, with God in their midst. In the final chapters of the book, part of next week's reading, Ezekiel receives a vision of a future temple of God and a restored, resettled land.

Read	Checkpoints
☑ Ezekiel 19–21	• two sisters
☑ Ezekiel 22–24	• an unusual mourning
☑ Ezekiel 25–27	• the watchman
☑ Ezekiel 28–30	• showers of blessing
☑ Ezekiel 31–33	• dry bones
☑ Ezekiel 34–36	
☑ Ezekiel 37–39	

First and foremost, God is the true hero of the story. No matter how captivating the other characters may be, our top priority is to discover what the Bible reveals about God.

—*Carolyn Custis James*

Share the Journey

How did you experience God's heart in this week's reading?

Something you learned or an insight you gained

A verse or passage you'd like to remember

Questions

08/07

stay true

The final chapters of Ezekiel look to the future. The letters of 1, 2, and 3 John and Jude turn to situations at the time they were written during the early years of the church.

The apostle John wrote the three letters that bear his name, and Jude, a brother of James (and half-brother of Jesus), wrote the letter of Jude. The letters all deal with church life. The situation prompting 3 John was a church leader abusing his authority. The other letters warn Christians to recognize and avoid false teachings and the teachers who promote them. Churches at this time commonly sent out and received traveling teachers. Some teachers, however, denied that Jesus had a physical body and actually suffered and died on the cross. Others promoted the idea that salvation came through special knowledge, not through Jesus, God's Son. John and Jude urged responding to false teaching by believing the truth about Jesus and living with love.

As a young teen, Daniel was taken captive to Babylon. He eventually became an advisor to Babylon's King Nebuchadnezzar and later to King Cyrus of Persia.

Read	Checkpoints
☑ Ezekiel 40–42	• our advocate
☑ Ezekiel 43–45	• children of God
☑ Ezekiel 46–48	• special-delivery faith
☑ 1 John 1–5	• four in a furnace
☑ 2 John, 3 John, Jude	• mysterious handwriting
☑ Daniel 1–3	
☑ Daniel 4–6	

God's Word isn't safe. I open the Bible with care because I know it can explode in my hands.

—*Pat Magness*

Share the Journey

How did you experience God's heart in this week's reading?

Something you learned or an insight you gained

A verse or passage you'd like to remember

Questions

08/14 +
zoom
BTS
(absent)

God reigns

The first six chapters of Daniel span much of Daniel's lifetime; his lions-den experience occurred when he was about eighty. The book's remaining chapters detail prophetic visions God gave to Daniel. These visions are apocalyptic, meaning that they use symbolic images and involve God's intervention in history to judge evil and establish eternal righteousness.

Most of the book of Revelation, the New Testament book of prophecy, is apocalyptic also. During the persecution of Christians by the Roman emperor Domitian, the apostle John was exiled on the small island of Patmos. There John received the visions recorded in Revelation—in chapters 1 through 3, a vision of Christ and messages from him for seven churches; in chapters 4 through 18, a view from heaven as events occur there and on earth; and in chapters 19 through 22, visions of the return of Christ, judgment, and the creation of a new heaven and a new earth.

Apocalyptic writing can be difficult to understand precisely. Various views for interpreting Revelation exist, but the book's primary intent is to assure believers that God is in control and that those who persevere will reign with Christ.

Read	Checkpoints
☑ Daniel 7–9	• seventy weeks
☑ Daniel 10–12 (12)	• the first and the last
☑ Revelation 1–3	• seven seals, trumpets, and bowls
☑ Revelation 4–6	• the angel with a little book
☑ Revelation 7–10	• witnesses and beasts
☑ Revelation 11–15	
☑ Revelation 16–18	

I've read the last page of the Bible. It's all going to turn out all right.

—Billy Graham

Share the Journey

How did you experience God's heart in this week's reading?

Something you learned or an insight you gained

A verse or passage you'd like to remember

Questions

08/21

lovers and locusts

The book of Hosea introduces a section of the Bible sometimes called the minor prophets, referring primarily to the shorter length of these books.

Hosea lived in the northern kingdom of Israel and prophesied during the eighth century BC. The kings of Israel had led the people into idol worship once again. God told Hosea to marry and have children as an object lesson. Hosea's wife, Gomer, might have been a prostitute at the time Hosea married her, or she might have become a prostitute after leaving Hosea. Either way, the marriage illustrates the relationship of God with his people and their treatment of him. The command for Hosea to find Gomer and take her back as his wife illustrates God's mercy and love for his people. In between, there would be the pain of bondage, however—Gomer to another man and Israel under Assyrian assault and rule.

Joel prophesied in Judah, probably earlier than Hosea. His book uses a devastating invasion of locusts to represent God's judgment unless the people turned their hearts back to God. Joel ends with assurances of future restoration and blessing.

Read	Checkpoints
☑ Revelation 19–22	• the river of life
☑ Hosea 1–3	• a hedge of thorns
☑ Hosea 4–6	• a roaring lion
☑ Hosea 7–9	• the Lord's army
☑ Hosea 10–12	• restored years
☑ Hosea 13–14	
☑ Joel 1–3	

The Word of God is a great deep. The commandment is exceeding broad. And so we cannot by merely occasional, hurried and perfunctory use of it understand its meaning and power.

—*John Murray*

Share the Journey

How did you experience God's heart in this week's reading?

Something you learned or an insight you gained

A verse or passage you'd like to remember

Questions

08/28
zoom

justice and a little town

Four more brought important messages to God's people. Amos prophesied in Israel during a time of prosperity for the upper class that in turn ignored the needs of the poor—even oppressing and cheating them—while pretending to worship God. Amos expressed God's concern for justice and moral living, but his message was rejected.

Obadiah's prophesy addressed the people of Edom, the descendants of Jacob's brother, Esau. Obadiah said God would judge Edom because they treated Israel, their relatives, as an enemy.

God called Jonah, a contemporary of Amos, to go to Nineveh, the capital city of Assyria, to warn of disaster unless they repented. Though the Ninevites had no relationship with God as the Israelites did, the entire city did repent—an event that should have been an object lesson for God's people.

Micah, a contemporary of Isaiah, warned that the cities of Samaria in the north and Jerusalem in the south both would fall. His prophecies alternate themes of judgment and redemption and the return of the exiles to their homeland. Micah also foretold the birthplace of the Savior—Bethlehem.

Read	Checkpoints
☑ Amos 1–3	• a plumb line
☑ Amos 4–6	• a man thrown overboard
☑ Amos 7–9	• a special fish
☑ Obadiah	• a withered plant
☑ Jonah 1–4	• a little town
☑ Micah 1–4	
☑ Micah 5–7	

Second Timothy 3:16 says, "All Scripture is God-breathed," so don't just read it like any other inspirational or instructional text. Inhale it!

—Beth Moore

Share the Journey

How did you experience God's heart in this week's reading?

Something you learned or an insight you gained

A verse or passage you'd like to remember

Questions

8/04

listen and respond

The Old Testament—and our year of reading through the Bible—closes with short messages from six additional prophets.

Nahum preached to the Assyrians in Nineveh a century after the fall of Samaria (capital of the northern kingdom). But this time they did not repent, and therefore, although God had used the Assyrians for his purposes, they would face his wrath for their own guilt. About the same time, in Judah, Habakkuk asked God questions and God answered. Zephaniah prophesied in Judah during the forty years before the fall of Jerusalem with a bad news-good news message, including a prophecy about Jesus.

Haggai encouraged the returned exiles to examine their hearts and rebuild the temple. Zechariah (a contemporary of Haggai) and Malachi also prophesied to the exiles. Zechariah's book contains apocalyptic visions like those of Daniel and Revelation and includes many prophecies of the Messiah. Malachi prophesied about one hundred years later, after temple worship had been restored for some time. In most of the book, God himself is speaking, calling his people to remember who he is and to live in genuine relationship with him.

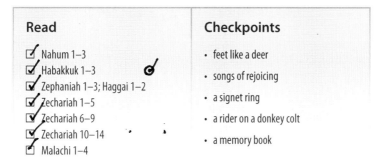

Read	Checkpoints
☑ Nahum 1–3	• feet like a deer
☑ Habakkuk 1–3	• songs of rejoicing
☑ Zephaniah 1–3; Haggai 1–2	• a signet ring
☑ Zechariah 1–5	• a rider on a donkey colt
☑ Zechariah 6–9	• a memory book
☑ Zechariah 10–14	
☑ Malachi 1–4	

God has placed all that you need to know about him between the covers of the Bible. But only you can open its pages to discover what he is saying to you.

—Once-A-Day Walk with Jesus Devotional, *June 28 reading,*

Share the Journey

How did you experience God's heart in this week's reading?

Something you learned or an insight you gained

A verse or passage you'd like to remember

Questions

a time line of Old Testament events

Creation	before recorded history
Flood	before recorded history
Tower of Babel	before recorded history
Birth of Abram	2167 BC
Abram begins travels	2096 BC
Birth of Isaac	2067 BC
Joseph is made governor of Egypt	1886 BC
Jacob and his family move to Egypt	1877 BC
Birth of Moses	1526 BC
Moses leads the Israelites out of Egypt	1446 BC
Moses receives the law on Mount Sinai	1446 BC
Joshua leads the Israelites into Canaan	1406 BC
Judges' rule begins in Israel	1385 BC
Saul becomes Israel's first king	1050 BC
Samuel anoints David	1025 BC
David begins to reign over the tribe of Judah	1010 BC
David becomes king over all Israel	1003 BC
Solomon begins to rule	970 BC
Dedication of the temple	959 BC
Solomon dies and Israel divides	930 BC
Fall of the northern kingdom to Assyria	722 BC
Fall of the southern kingdom to Babylon	586 BC
First exiles return to Jerusalem	538 BC
Work begins to rebuild the temple	536 BC
Nehemiah leads the rebuilding of Jerusalem's walls	c. 445 BC

a time line of New Testament events

Birth of John the Baptist	6–5 BC
Birth of Jesus	6–4 BC
John baptizes Jesus	AD 26
Peter, James, and John witness the transfiguration	AD 29
Death, burial, and resurrection of Jesus	AD 30
The Holy Spirit comes at Pentecost	AD 30
Paul meets Jesus on the Damascus Road	c. AD 35
Paul's first missionary journey	AD 47–49
The council in Jerusalem	AD 51
Paul's second missionary journey	AD 52–54
Paul's third missionary journey	AD 54–58
Paul lives under house arrest in Rome	AD 61–63
John writes Revelation while exiled on Patmos	c. AD 95

Dates in these time lines are taken from *Discovering God's Story* (Cincinnati, OH: Standard Publishing, 2010).

reading plan

WEEK 1
- [ ] Genesis 1–3
- [ ] Genesis 4–6
- [ ] Genesis 7–9
- [ ] Genesis 10–12
- [ ] Genesis 13–15
- [ ] Genesis 16–18
- [ ] Genesis 19–21

WEEK 2
- [ ] Genesis 22–24
- [ ] Genesis 25–27
- [ ] Genesis 28–30
- [ ] Genesis 31–33
- [ ] Genesis 34–36
- [ ] Genesis 37–39
- [ ] Genesis 40–42

WEEK 3
- [ ] Genesis 43–45
- [ ] Genesis 46–50
- [ ] Matthew 1–3
- [ ] Matthew 4–6
- [ ] Matthew 7–9
- [ ] Matthew 10–12
- [ ] Matthew 13–15

WEEK 4
- [ ] Matthew 16–18
- [ ] Matthew 19–21
- [ ] Matthew 22–25
- [ ] Matthew 26–28
- [ ] Exodus 1–3
- [ ] Exodus 4–6
- [ ] Exodus 7–9

WEEK 5
- [ ] Exodus 10–12
- [ ] Exodus 13–15
- [ ] Exodus 16–18
- [ ] Exodus 19–21
- [ ] Exodus 22–24
- [ ] Exodus 25–27
- [ ] Exodus 28–30

WEEK 6
- [ ] Exodus 31–33
- [ ] Exodus 34–36
- [ ] Exodus 37–40
- [ ] Mark 1–3
- [ ] Mark 4–6
- [ ] Mark 7–9
- [ ] Mark 10–12

WEEK 7
- [ ] Mark 13–16
- [ ] Leviticus 1–3
- [ ] Leviticus 4–6
- [ ] Leviticus 7–9
- [ ] Leviticus 10–12
- [ ] Leviticus 13–15
- [ ] Leviticus 16–18

WEEK 8
- [ ] Leviticus 19–21
- [ ] Leviticus 22–24
- [ ] Leviticus 25–27
- [ ] Luke 1–3
- [ ] Luke 4–6
- [ ] Luke 7–9
- [ ] Luke 10–12

WEEK 9
- [ ] Luke 13–15
- [ ] Luke 16–18
- [ ] Luke 19–21
- [ ] Luke 22–24
- [ ] Numbers 1–3
- [ ] Numbers 4–6
- [ ] Numbers 7–9

WEEK 10
- [ ] Numbers 10–12
- [ ] Numbers 13–15
- [ ] Numbers 16–18
- [ ] Numbers 19–21
- [ ] Numbers 22–24
- [ ] Numbers 25–27
- [ ] Numbers 28–30

WEEK 11
- [ ] Numbers 31–33
- [ ] Numbers 34–36
- [ ] John 1–3
- [ ] John 4–6
- [ ] John 7–9
- [ ] John 10–12
- [ ] John 13–15

WEEK 12
- [ ] John 16–18
- [ ] John 19–21
- [ ] Deuteronomy 1–3
- [ ] Deuteronomy 4–6
- [ ] Deuteronomy 7–9
- [ ] Deuteronomy 10–12
- [ ] Deuteronomy 13–15

WEEK 13
- [ ] Deuteronomy 16–18
- [ ] Deuteronomy 19–21
- [ ] Deuteronomy 22–24
- [ ] Deuteronomy 25–27
- [ ] Deuteronomy 28–30
- [ ] Deuteronomy 31–34
- [ ] Psalms 1–5

WEEK 14
- [ ] Psalms 6–10
- [ ] Psalms 11–15
- [ ] Psalms 16–20
- [ ] Psalms 21–25
- [ ] Psalms 26–30
- [ ] Psalms 31–34
- [ ] Psalms 35–37

WEEK 15
- [ ] Psalms 38–41
- [ ] Acts 1–3
- [ ] Acts 4–6
- [ ] Acts 7–9
- [ ] Acts 10–12
- [ ] Acts 13–15
- [ ] Acts 16–18

WEEK 16
- [ ] Acts 19–21
- [ ] Acts 22–24
- [ ] Acts 25–28
- [ ] Joshua 1–3
- [ ] Joshua 4–6
- [ ] Joshua 7–9
- [ ] Joshua 10–12

WEEK 17
- [ ] Joshua 13–15
- [ ] Joshua 16–18
- [ ] Joshua 19–21
- [ ] Joshua 22–24
- [ ] Romans 1–3
- [ ] Romans 4–6
- [ ] Romans 7–9

WEEK 18
- [ ] Romans 10–12
- [ ] Romans 13–16
- [ ] Judges 1–3
- [ ] Judges 4–6
- [ ] Judges 7–9
- [ ] Judges 10–12
- [ ] Judges 13–16

WEEK 19
- [ ] Judges 17–19
- [ ] Judges 20–21
- [ ] Ruth 1–4
- [ ] 1 Corinthians 1–2
- [ ] 1 Corinthians 3–4
- [ ] 1 Corinthians 5–6
- [ ] 1 Corinthians 7–9

WEEK 20
- [ ] 1 Corinthians 10–13
- [ ] 1 Corinthians 14–16
- [ ] 1 Samuel 1–3
- [ ] 1 Samuel 4–6
- [ ] 1 Samuel 7–9
- [ ] 1 Samuel 10–12
- [ ] 1 Samuel 13–15

WEEK 21
- [ ] 1 Samuel 16–18
- [ ] 1 Samuel 19–21
- [ ] 1 Samuel 22–24
- [ ] 1 Samuel 25–27
- [ ] 1 Samuel 28–31
- [ ] 2 Corinthians 1–3
- [ ] 2 Corinthians 4–6

WEEK 22
- [ ] 2 Corinthians 7–9
- [ ] 2 Corinthians 10–13
- [ ] 2 Samuel 1–3
- [ ] 2 Samuel 4–6
- [ ] 2 Samuel 7–9
- [ ] 2 Samuel 10–12
- [ ] 2 Samuel 13–15

WEEK 23
- [ ] 2 Samuel 16–18
- [ ] 2 Samuel 19–21
- [ ] 2 Samuel 22–24
- [ ] Galatians 1–3
- [ ] Galatians 4–6
- [ ] 1 Kings 1–3
- [ ] 1 Kings 4–6

WEEK 24
- [ ] 1 Kings 7–9
- [ ] 1 Kings 10–12
- [ ] 1 Kings 13–15
- [ ] 1 Kings 16–18
- [ ] 1 Kings 19–22
- [ ] Ephesians 1–3
- [ ] Ephesians 4–6

WEEK 25
- [ ] 2 Kings 1–3
- [ ] 2 Kings 4–7
- [ ] 2 Kings 8–10
- [ ] 2 Kings 11–14
- [ ] 2 Kings 15–17
- [ ] 2 Kings 18–21
- [ ] 2 Kings 22–25

WEEK 26
- [ ] Philippians 1–4
- [ ] Psalms 42–45
- [ ] Psalms 46–49
- [ ] Psalms 50–53
- [ ] Psalms 54–57
- [ ] Psalms 58–61
- [ ] Psalms 62–66

WEEK 27
- [ ] Psalms 67–69
- [ ] Psalms 70–72
- [ ] 1 Chronicles 1–3
- [ ] 1 Chronicles 4–6
- [ ] 1 Chronicles 7–9
- [ ] 1 Chronicles 10–12
- [ ] 1 Chronicles 13–15

WEEK 28
- [ ] 1 Chronicles 16–18
- [ ] 1 Chronicles 19–22
- [ ] 1 Chronicles 23–26
- [ ] 1 Chronicles 27–29
- [ ] Colossians 1–4
- [ ] 2 Chronicles 1–3
- [ ] 2 Chronicles 4–6

WEEK 29
- [ ] 2 Chronicles 7–9
- [ ] 2 Chronicles 10–12
- [ ] 2 Chronicles 13–15
- [ ] 2 Chronicles 16–18
- [ ] 2 Chronicles 19–21
- [ ] 2 Chronicles 22–24
- [ ] 2 Chronicles 25–27

WEEK 30
- [ ] 2 Chronicles 28–30
- [ ] 2 Chronicles 31–33
- [ ] 2 Chronicles 34–36
- [ ] 1 Thessalonians 1–5
- [ ] 2 Thessalonians 1–3
- [ ] Ezra 1–3
- [ ] Ezra 4–6

WEEK 31
- [ ] Ezra 7–10
- [ ] Nehemiah 1–3
- [ ] Nehemiah 4–6
- [ ] Nehemiah 7–9
- [ ] Nehemiah 10–13
- [ ] Esther 1–3
- [ ] Esther 4–6

WEEK 32
- [ ] Esther 7–10
- [ ] 1 Timothy 1–3
- [ ] 1 Timothy 4–6
- [ ] 2 Timothy 1–4
- [ ] Job 1–4
- [ ] Job 5–8
- [ ] Job 9–12

WEEK 33
☐ Job 13–16
☐ Job 17–21
☐ Job 22–26
☐ Job 27–30
☐ Job 31–34
☐ Job 35–38
☐ Job 39–42

WEEK 34
☐ Psalms 73–76
☐ Psalms 77–78
☐ Psalms 79–82
☐ Psalms 83–86
☐ Psalms 87–89
☐ Psalms 90–93
☐ Psalms 94–97

WEEK 35
☐ Psalms 98–102
☐ Psalms 103–104
☐ Psalms 105–106
☐ Titus 1–3, Philemon
☐ Proverbs 1–4
☐ Proverbs 5–8
☐ Proverbs 9–12

WEEK 36
☐ Proverbs 13–15
☐ Proverbs 16–17
☐ Proverbs 18–20
☐ Proverbs 21–23
☐ Proverbs 24–26
☐ Proverbs 27–29
☐ Proverbs 30–31

WEEK 37
☐ Hebrews 1–4
☐ Hebrews 5–7
☐ Hebrews 8–10
☐ Hebrews 11–13
☐ Ecclesiastes 1–3
☐ Ecclesiastes 4–6
☐ Ecclesiastes 7–9

WEEK 38
☐ Ecclesiastes 10–12
☐ Song of Solomon 1–2
☐ Song of Solomon 3–5
☐ Song of Solomon 6–8
☐ James 1–5
☐ Isaiah 1–3
☐ Isaiah 4–7

WEEK 39
☐ Isaiah 8–10
☐ Isaiah 11–13
☐ Isaiah 14–17
☐ Isaiah 18–21
☐ Isaiah 22–25
☐ Isaiah 26–28
☐ Isaiah 29–30

WEEK 40
☐ Isaiah 31–33
☐ Isaiah 34–36
☐ Isaiah 37–39
☐ Isaiah 40–42
☐ Isaiah 43–45
☐ Isaiah 46–48
☐ Isaiah 49–51

WEEK 41
☐ Isaiah 52–54
☐ Isaiah 55–57
☐ Isaiah 58–60
☐ Isaiah 61–63
☐ Isaiah 64–66
☐ 1 Peter 1–5
☐ 2 Peter 1–3

WEEK 42
☐ Jeremiah 1–3
☐ Jeremiah 4–6
☐ Jeremiah 7–9
☐ Jeremiah 10–12
☐ Jeremiah 13–15
☐ Jeremiah 16–18
☐ Jeremiah 19–21

WEEK 43
☐ Jeremiah 22–23
☐ Jeremiah 24–26
☐ Jeremiah 27–29
☐ Jeremiah 30–31
☐ Jeremiah 32–33
☐ Jeremiah 34–36
☐ Jeremiah 37–39

WEEK 44
☐ Jeremiah 40–43
☐ Jeremiah 44–48
☐ Jeremiah 49–52
☐ Lamentations 1–2
☐ Lamentations 3–5
☐ Psalms 107–109
☐ Psalms 110–115

WEEK 45
☐ Psalms 116–118
☐ Psalm 119:1–88
☐ Psalm 119:89–176
☐ Psalms 120–127
☐ Psalms 128–134
☐ Psalms 135–138
☐ Psalms 139–142

WEEK 46
☐ Psalms 143–146
☐ Psalms 147–150
☐ Ezekiel 1–4
☐ Ezekiel 5–8
☐ Ezekiel 9–12
☐ Ezekiel 13–15
☐ Ezekiel 16–18

WEEK 47
☐ Ezekiel 19–21
☐ Ezekiel 22–24
☐ Ezekiel 25–27
☐ Ezekiel 28–30
☐ Ezekiel 31–33
☐ Ezekiel 34–36
☐ Ezekiel 37–39

WEEK 48
☐ Ezekiel 40–42
☐ Ezekiel 43–45
☐ Ezekiel 46–48
☐ 1 John 1–5
☐ 2 John, 3 John, Jude
☐ Daniel 1–3
☐ Daniel 4–6

WEEK 49
☐ Daniel 7–9
☐ Daniel 10–12
☐ Revelation 1–3
☐ Revelation 4–6
☐ Revelation 7–10
☐ Revelation 11–15
☐ Revelation 16–18

WEEK 50
☐ Revelation 19–22
☐ Hosea 1–3
☐ Hosea 4–6
☐ Hosea 7–9
☐ Hosea 10–12
☐ Hosea 13–14
☐ Joel 1–3

WEEK 51
☐ Amos 1–3
☐ Amos 4–6
☐ Amos 7–9
☐ Obadiah
☐ Jonah 1–4
☐ Micah 1–4
☐ Micah 5–7

WEEK 52
☐ Nahum 1–3
☐ Habakkuk 1–3
☐ Zephaniah 1–3, Haggai 1–2
☐ Zechariah 1–5
☐ Zechariah 6–9
☐ Zechariah 10–14
☐ Malachi 1–4

resources

Your Bible, this guidebook, and the insights of other women are all you really need for your life-changing journey into the heart of God. But if you find there's a topic you want to know more about, use this list to find other resources to enhance your study.

Books

Bible dictionaries (more like compact encyclopedias) and handbooks provide background on Bible books, events, people, and places as well as the culture and customs of Bible times. *The Revell Bible Dictionary: Deluxe Color Edition*, edited by Lawrence O. Richards, is my favorite. This 1994 publication is out of print, but well worth the search for a used copy. It's a treasure. Newer Bible dictionaries include the *Holman Illustrated Bible Dictionary* (2003), the *Zondervan Illustrated Bible Dictionary* (2011), and *The International Standard Bible Encyclopedia* (2010, available in a Kindle edition without illustrations). I also have enjoyed the *Zondervan Handbook to the Bible* (1973, 2002).

Before online word searches were possible, a Bible concordance was the easiest way to track down all the uses of a particular word in the Bible. Your Bible might include an abbreviated concordance. If you prefer to purchase a separate concordance, try to match it with the version of the Bible you are reading.

Many Bibles include some maps, but if geography interests you, a Bible atlas will too, helping you place where Bible people lived and traveled and where events took place. The *Deluxe Then and Now Bible Maps* from Rose Publishing is one option.

Websites and Apps

With these online tools and apps for mobile devices, you can look up specific passages and search for specific words in multiple Bible versions, read commentaries and dictionaries, view maps, find devotionals and other reading plans, and so much more.

BibleGateway.com
BibleStudyTools.com
BlueLetterBible.org
Bible360.com
YouVersion.com

DVD

The Bible Collection, 2005, six DVDs available as a set or individually:

Abraham, Jacob, Joseph, Moses, David, Samson and Delilah

Also available:

Esther (2000)
Jeremiah (1998)

Note: Read online reviews and preview these or any other DVDs before a group showing.

references

Week	Source of Quotation

1   Catherine Martin, *Knowing and Loving the Bible* (Eugene, OR: Harvest House Publishers, 2007), 83. http://tinyurl.com/7z6qfuw

2   *The Poetical Works of William Cowper*, vol. 2 (London: William Smith, 1839), 114. http://tinyurl.com/7nf2rrn

3   www.brainyquote.com/quotes/quotes/m/martinluth165433.html

4   Margaret Feinberg, *Scouting the Divine* (Grand Rapids, MI: Zondervan, 2009), 9. www.amazon.com/dp/0310291224/ref=rdr_ext_tmb

5   Catherine Mackenzie, ed., *What the Bible Means to Me: Testimonies of How God's Word Impacts Lives* (Scotland: Christian Focus Publications, 2011), 132.

6   http://dailychristianquote.com/dcqbible4.html

7   www.brainyquote.com/quotes/quotes/d/dwightlmo157627.html

8   http://mywingsaremadeoffaith.typepad.com/faith/2011/10/an-open-letter-to-the-thief.html

9   http://bibleresources.org/bibleresources/bible-quotes/

10   http://bibleresources.org/bibleresources/bible-quotes/

11   http://kellerquotes.com/all-about-jesus/

12   http://dailychristianquote.com/dcqguidance3.html

13   Catherine Mackenzie, ed., *What the Bible Means to Me: Testimonies of How God's Word Impacts Lives* (Scotland: Christian Focus Publications, 2011), 112.

14   http://christianstandard.com/2011/09/a-stormy-and-sweet-romance/ (9-16-11 print issue)

15   www.tentmaker.org/Quotes/biblequotes.htm

16   www.tentmaker.org/Quotes/biblequotes.htm

17   Catherine Mackenzie, ed., *What the Bible Means to Me: Testimonies of How God's Word Impacts Lives* (Scotland: Christian Focus Publications, 2011), 8.

18   www.reviveourhearts.com/radio/revive-our-hearts/alphabet-prayers/

19   www.brainyquote.com/quotes/quotes/h/helenkelle152190.html

20   www.brainyquote.com/quotes/quotes/e/elizabethi389118.html

21   www.brainyquote.com/quotes/quotes/w/williamlyo385573.html

22   Martin H. Manser, compiler, *The Westminster Collection of Christian Quotations* (Louisville, KY: Westminster John Knox Press, 2001), 248. http://tinyurl.com/72c753g

Week	Source of Quotation

23 Priscilla Shirer, *Discerning the Voice of God* (Chicago: Moody, 2007, 2012), 162.

24 John Piper on Twitter, January 20, 2012. https://twitter.com/#!/JohnPiper

25 http://dailychristianquote.com/dcqbible4.html

26 www.spurgeon.us/mind_and_heart/quotes/b2.htm

27 http://lysaterkeurst.com/2011/09/my-jesus-in-5-days/

28 www.faithvillage.com/2012/01/no-girls-allowed-sandra-glahn/

29 www.tentmaker.org/Quotes/biblequotes.htm

30 www.bible-history.com/quotes/henry_h_haley_1.html

31 http://multnomahemails.com/wbmlt/pdf/BibleStudyFAQ.pdf

32 Dr. Henry Cloud and Dr. John Townsend, *How People Grow* (Grand Rapids, MI: Zondervan, 2001), 191.

33 http://jcrylequotes.com/2012/02/13/prize-the-bible-more-and-more/

34 http://blog.christianitytoday.com/women/2012/02/seeing_jesus_in_the_old_testam_1.html

35 http://christianstandard.com/2011/02/nancy-meets-god-in-isaiah/

36 www.aholyexperience.com/2010/03/best-read-ever/

37 www.reviveourhearts.com/radio/revive-our-hearts/light/

38 http://thegospelcoalition.org/blogs/rayortlund/2012/03/08/the-longer-i-live/

39 Elisabeth Elliot, *Passion and Purity* (Grand Rapids, MI: Revell, 1984, 2002), 87.

40 Quoted by Lawrence Kimbrough, *Words to Die For* (Nashville: Broadman & Holman, 2002), 167–168.

41 www.facebook.com/WhatsintheBible/posts/10150103379766835 and others: http://tinyurl.com/capefka

42 *The Prayer of the Lord* www.goodreads.com/work/quotes/6606279-the-prayer-of-the-lord

43 www.goodreads.com/quotes/tag/bible?page=5

44 www.goodreads.com/author/quotes/36835.Ruth-Bell-Graham

45 http://dailychristianquote.com/dcqtada.html

46 www.frankjuelich.in/Illustrations%20-%20B.htm

47 www.goodreads.com/author/quotes/52039.Carolyn.Custis.James

48 http://christianstandard.com/2011/03/a-dangerous-book/

49 www.brainyquote.com/quotes/keywords/bible.html

50 "The Study of the Bible" in *The Collected Writings of John Murray*, vol. 1 (Carlisle, PA: Banner of Truth, 1991), 3–4.

51 Beth Moore, *Believing God* (Nashville, B&H Publishing Group, 2004), 128. http://tinyurl.com/cwkrkl2

52 Walk Thru the Bible Ministries, *Once-A-Day Walk with Jesus Devotional* (Grand Rapids, MI: Zondervan, 2011). http://tinyurl.com/bm5j274

acknowledgments

To Beth Hawkins Neuenschwander, who opened her home every Monday night for more than ten years so women like me could discover the treasure in reading through the Bible in a year—thank you.

To all the Monday night Bible study women who shared the journey with me through the years, and especially those in my group in 2012: Jessie Spikes, Linda Long, Lynn Pratt, Lynn Rodenbeck, and Marlene Gresham—thank you.

To the friends who prayed for me while I wrote and who encouraged me through all the obstacles—thank you.

To my husband, Ed, for his great patience and support—thank you.

To Dr. William R. Baker, professor of New Testament at Hope International University in Fullerton, California, for reviewing the New Testament commentary, and to Cheryl Frey for eagle-eyed help and suggestions regarding the Old Testament commentary—thank you.

To my agent before her retirement, Etta G. Wilson, for believing in me even before I realized what I wanted to do—thank you.

To Janet Kobobel Grant, my agent with Books & Such Literary Agency, who got excited about this project when she heard me speak at Mount Hermon—thank you.

To my editor, Andy McGuire, and to the entire Bethany House team for understanding my dream for what this book could be and for your suggestions to make it even better—thank you.

Now all glory to God, who is able, through his mighty power at work within us, to accomplish infinitely more than we might ask or think. Glory to him in the church and in Christ Jesus through all generations forever and ever! Amen.

Ephesians 3:20–21

about the author

Diane Stortz has been involved with publishing for many years as an editor, editorial director, and author. Her children's books include the bestselling *The Sweetest Story Bible* (Zondervan), *Thankful for God's Blessings* (Ideals), *Rumble! Zap! Pow! Mighty Stories of God* (Tyndale), and *Jesus Loves You: A Read the Pictures Book* (Standard).

She is cofounder of the National Network of Parents of Missionaries and coauthor of *Parents of Missionaries: How to Thrive and Stay Connected When Your Children and Grandchildren Serve Cross-Culturally* (IVP).

Diane and her husband, Ed, have two married daughters and five grandsons. They live in Cincinnati, Ohio.

Visit Diane at DianeStortz.com and ChristianChildrens Authors.com.